THE PATROL FRIGATE STORY

The Tacoma-class Frigates
in World War II and the Korean War
1943-1953

David Hendrickson

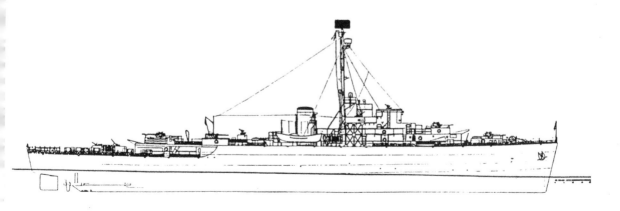

THE PATROL FRIGATE STORY

The Tacoma-class Frigates in World War II and the Korean War 1943-1953

By David Hendrickson

Jacksonville, Florida ♦ Herndon, Virginia

www.Fortis-Publishing.com

THE PATROL FRIGATE STORY

The Tacoma-class Frigates in World War II and the Korean War 1943-1953

By David Hendrickson

ISBN 978-0-984XXXXXX (trade paperback version)

Published by Fortis Publishing

Jacksonville, Florida—Herndon, Virginia

www.Fortis-Publishing.com

Manufactured in the United States of America

DEDICATION

To all hands who served on the patrol
frigates of WWII and the Korean War.

A Sailor's Best Friend --Frigate Fleet "Sea Dogs"

Butch -- Groton (PF-29)

Musky -- Muskogee (PF-49)

Soogey -- Sandusky (PF-54)

Bomber -- Brownsville (PF-10)

Salty -- Newport (PF-27)

Spunky -- Albuquerque (PF-7)

Tuffy -- Everett (PF-8)

TABLE OF CONTENTS

TABLE OF CONTENTS (CONTINUED)

FOREWORD AND ACKNOWLEDGEMENTS

In this short account, I have done my best to reconstruct the role of the patrol frigates of World War II and, briefly, the Korean War. The singular purpose has been to preserve in memory the "Forgotten Fleet," seventy-five patrol /escort/ASW vessels manned by the Coast Guard in WWII in waters from the frozen Arctic to the steamy tropics. I have attempted a balanced coverage; however, all errors, omissions and charges of unbalanced treatment discovered by old seadogs must land on my doorstep and mine alone. The account would not have seen the light of day without the urging insistence of Patrol Frigate Reunion Association chairman, Roberta Shotwell, and her willingness to collect stories, photos, logs and memories and to glean choice features from past PFRA Bulletins. Not the least, my deepest thanks expressed here to the gallant contributors who answered the appeal in the Bulletin and sent thick envelopes and brown packets of invaluable materials.

DHH

Jim Matlock PF-38

Dale Benson PF-48

Jack Chambers PF-6

Roland Schreiter PF-4

Milton Woodruff PF-63

Steave Irgens PF-19

Jim Lily PF-37

Joe Brogan PF-60

George Harris PF-45

Paul Woods PF-101

Dick Hofmaster PF-35

Richard Duberg PF-63

Frank Intigliatta PF-29

Richard Greer PF-55

Virgil Davis PF-49

Bob Johnson PF-40

Louis Gamba PF-39

Russel Hitchens PF-42

John Buscemi PF-32

Dean Scholl PF-15

Stan Sage PF-51

Art Wells PF-35

Kim Berry PF-8

Wiliam Deyoe PF-61

Harry Morgan PF-14

Owen Cresap PF-15

Bill McShane PF-29

Bob Krayer PF-58

George Bock PF-100

Earl Day PF-3

Tom Sargent PF-54

Casper Fries PF-40

Bob DeWitt PF-12

Ed Baehr PF-54

John Horne PF-10

Frank Seigal PF-52

Wilbur Sharick PF-45

Peter Kopchik PF-47

John Johnson PF-8

Dick Irussi PF-24

Al Larsen PF-70

George Kopres PF-29

U.S. Coast Guard-Manned Patrol Frigates of World War II

USS Tacoma PF-3
USS Sausalito PF-4
USS Hoquiam PF-5
USS Pasco PF-6
USS Albuquerque PF-7
USS Everett PF-8
USS Pocatello PF-9
USS Brownsville PF-10
USS Grand Forks PF-11
USS Casper PF-12
USS Pueblo PF-13
USS Grand Island PF-14
USS Annapolis PF-15
USS Bangor PF-16
USS Key West PF-17
USS Alexandria PF-18
USS Huron PF-19
USS Gulfport PF-20
USS Bayonne PF-21
USS Gloucester PF-22
USS Shreveport PF-23
USS Muskegon PF-24
USS Charlottesville PF-25
USS Poughkeepsie PF-26
USS Newport PF-27
USS Emporia PF-28
USS Groton PF-29
USS Hingham PF-30
USS Grand Rapids PF-31
USS Woonsocket PF-32
USS Dearborn PF-33
USS Long Beach PF-34
USS Belfast PF-35
USS Glendale PF-36
USS San Pedro PF-37
USS Coronado PF-38
USS Ogden PF-39
USS Eugene PF-40

USS El Paso PF-41
USS Van Buren PF-42
USS Orange PF-43
USS Corpus Christi PF-44
USS Hutchinson PF-45
USS Bisbee PF-46
USS Gallup PF-47
USS Rockford PF-48
USS Muskogee PF-49
USS Carson City PF-50
USS Burlington PF-51
USS Allentown PF-52
USS Machias PF-53
USS Sandusky PF-54
USS Bath PF-55
USS Covington PF-56
USS Sheboygan PF-57
USS Abilene PF-58
USS Beaufort PF-59
USS Charlotte PF-60
USS Manitowoc PF-61
USS Gladwyne PF-62
USS Moberly PF-63
USS Knoxville PF-64
USS Uniontown PF-65
USS Reading PF-66
USS Peoria PF-67
USS Brunswick PF-68
USS Davenport PF-69
USS Evansville PF-70
USS New Bedford PF-71
USS Lorain PF-93
USS Milledgeville PF-94
USS Orlando PF-99
USS Racine PF-100
USS Greensboro PF-101
USS Forsyth PF-102

PATROL FRIGATES

ASHEVILLE and TACOMA classes

Displacement:	1509t (*Natchez* 1412t) standard; 2238t (*Long Beach* 2230t) full load
Dimensions:	*Asheville* class: 283ft wl, 301ft 6in × 36ft 6in × 13ft 2in full load 86.25, 91.90 × 11.13 × 4.01m *Tacoma* class: 285ft 6in wl, 303 ft 11in oa × 37ft 6in × 12ft 8in 87.02, 92.63 × 11.43 × 3.86m
Machinery:	2-shaft VTE, 3 boilers, 5500ihp = 20kts. Oil 674t (*Tacoma* class 768t), range 9500nm at 12kts (*Tacoma* class – unofficial)
Armament:	3–3in/50, 4–40mm (2×2), 9–20mm (4–20mm in *Asheville*s, 2–3in/50, 4–40mm, 4–20mm in weather ships), 1 Hedgehog, 8 DC projectors, 2 DC racks
Complement:	190 (weather ships 176)

No.	Name	Builder	Launched	Fate
PF1	ASHEVILLE (ex-HMS *Adur*)	Canadian Vickers	22.8.1942	To Argentina June 1946
PF2	NATCHEZ (ex-HMS *Annan*)	Canadian Vickers	12.9.1942	To Dominican Republic July 1947
PF3	TACOMA	Kaiser, Richmond	7.7.1943	To S Korea Oct 1951
PF4	SAUSALITO	Kaiser, Richmond	20.7.1943	To S Korea 1953
PF5	HOQUIAM	Kaiser, Richmond	31.7.1943	To S Korea Oct 1951
PF6	PASCO	Kaiser, Richmond	17.8.1943	To Japan 1953
PF7	ALBUQUERQUE	Kaiser, Richmond	14.9.1943	To Japan 1953
PF8	EVERETT	Kaiser, Richmond	29.9.1943	To Japan Mar 1953
PF9	POCATELLO	Kaiser, Richmond	17.10.1943	Sold Sept 1947
PF10	BROWNSVILLE	Kaiser, Richmond	14.11.1943	Sold Sept 1947
PF11	GRAND FORKS	Kaiser, Richmond	27.11.1943	Sold May 1947
PF12	CASPER	Kaiser, Richmond	27.12.1943	Sold May 1947
PF13	PUEBLO	Kaiser, Richmond	20.1.1944	To Dominican Republic Sept 1947
PF14	GRAND ISLAND	Kaiser, Richmond	19.2.1944	To Cuba June 1947
PF15	ANNAPOLIS	American SB, Lorain	16.10.1943	To Mexico Nov 1947
PF16	BANGOR	American SB, Lorain	6.11.1943	To Mexico Nov 1947
PF17	KEY WEST	American SB, Lorain	29.12.1943	Sold May 1947
PF18	ALEXANDRIA	American SB, Lorain	15.1.1944	BU 1947
PF19	HURON	American Cleveland	3.7.1943	Sold 1948
PF20	GULFPORT	American Cleveland	21.8.1943	BU 1947
PF21	BAYONNE	American Cleveland	11.9.1943	To Japan 1953
PF22	GLOUCESTER	Walter Butler, Superior	12.7.1943	To Japan 1953
PF23	SHREVEPORT	Walter Butler, Superior	15.7.1943	BU 1947
PF24	MUSKEGON	Walter Butler, Superior	25.7.1943	To France Mar 1947
PF25	CHARLOTTES-VILLE	Walter Butler, Superior	30.7.1943	To Japan Jan 1953
PF26	POUGHKEEPSIE	Walter Butler, Superior	12.8.1943	To Japan 1953
PF27	NEWPORT	Walter Butler, Superior	15.8.1943	To Japan 1953
PF28	EMPORIA	Walter Butler, Superior	30.8.1943	To France Mar 1947
PF29	GROTON	Walter Butler, Superior	14.9.1943	To Colombia Mar 1947
PF30	HINGHAM	Walter Butler, Superior	27.8.1943	BU 1947
PF31	GRAND RAPIDS	Walter Butler, Superior	10.9.1943	BU 1947
PF32	WOONSOCKET	Walter Butler, Superior	27.9.1943	To Peru Sept 1948
PF33	DEARBORN (ex-*Toledo*)	Walter Butler, Superior	27.9.1943	Sold July 1947
PF34	LONG BEACH	Consolidated Steel, San Pedro	5.5.1943	To Japan 1953
PF35	BELFAST	Consolidated Steel, San Pedro	20.5.1943	Lost 17.11.48
PF36	GLENDALE	Consolidated Steel, San Pedro	28.5.1943	To Thailand 1951
PF37	SAN PEDRO	Consolidated Steel, San Pedro	11.6.1943	To Japan 1953
PF38	CORONADO	Consolidated Steel, San Pedro	17.6.1943	To Japan Jan 1953
PF39	OGDEN	Consolidated Steel, San Pedro	23.6.1943	To Japan 1953
PF40	EUGENE	Consolidated Steel, San Pedro	6.7.1943	To Cuba June 1947
PF41	EL PASO	Consolidated Steel, San Pedro	16.7.1943	Sold Oct 1947
PF42	VAN BUREN	Consolidated Steel, San Pedro	27.7.1943	BU 1947
PF43	ORANGE	Consolidated Steel, San Pedro	6.8.1943	Sold Sept 1947
PF44	CORPUS CHRISTIE	Consolidated Steel, San Pedro	17.8.1943	Sold Oct 1947
PF45	HUTCHINSON	Consolidated Steel, San Pedro	27.8.1943	To Mexico Nov 1947
PF46	BISBEE	Consolidated Steel, San Pedro	7.9.1943	To Colombia Feb 1952
PF47	GALLUP	Consolidated Steel, San Pedro	17.9.1943	To Thailand Oct 1951
PF48	ROCKFORD	Consolidated Steel, San Pedro	27.9.1943	To S Korea Nov 1950

No	Name	Builder	Launched	Fate
PF49	MUSKOGEE	Consolidated Steel, San Pedro	18.10.1943	To S Korea Nov 1950
PF50	CARSON CITY	Consolidated Steel, San Pedro	13.11.1943	To Japan Apr 1953
PF51	BURLINGTON	Consolidated Steel, San Pedro	7.12.1943	To Colombia 1953
PF52	ALLENTOWN	Froemming Milwaukee	3.7.1943	To Japan Apr 1953
PF53	MACHIAS	Froemming Milwaukee	22.8.1943	To Japan 1953
PF54	SANDUSKY	Froemming Milwaukee	5.10.1943	To Japan 1953
PF55	BATH	Froemming Milwaukee	14.11.1943	To Japan Dec 1953
PF56	COVINGTON	Globe, Superior	15.7.1943	To Ecuador Aug 1947
PF57	SHEBOYGAN	Globe, Superior	31.7.1943	To Belgium Mar 1947
PF58	ABILENE (ex-Bridgeport)	Globe, Superior	21.8.1943	To Holland May 1947
PF59	BEAUFORT	Globe, Superior	9.10.1943	BU 1947
PF60	CHARLOTTE	Globe, Superior	10.10.1943	To mercantile service 1948
PF61	MANITOWOC	Globe, Duluth	30.11.1943	To France Mar 1947
PF62	GLADWYNE (ex-Worcester)	Globe, Duluth	7.1.1944	To Mexico Nov 1947
PF63	MOBERLY (ex-Scranton)	Globe, Duluth	26.1.1944	Sold Dec 1947
PF64	KNOXVILLE	Leatham D Smith SB, Superior	10.7.1943	To Dominican Republic Sept 1947
PF65	UNIONTOWN (ex-Chattanooga)	Leatham D Smith SB, Superior	7.8.1943	To Argentina June 1946
PF66	READING	Leatham D Smith SB, Superior	28.8.1943	To Argentina June 1946
PF67	PEORIA	Leatham D Smith SB, Superior	2.10.1943	To Cuba June 1947
PF68	BRUNSWICK	Leatham D Smith SB, Superior	6.11.1943	BU 1947
PF69	DAVENPORT	Leatham D Smith SB, Superior	8.12.1943	Sold June 1946
PF70	EVANSVILLE	Leatham D Smith SB, Superior	27.11.1943	To Japan Oct 1953
PF71	NEW BEDFORD	Leatham D Smith SB, Superior	29.12.1943	Sold Nov 1947
PF93	LORAIN (ex-Roanoke)	American SB, Lorain	18.3.1944	To France Mar 1947
PF94	MILLEDGEVILLE (ex-Sitka)	American SB, Lorain	5.4.1944	Sold Apr 1947
PF95	STAMFORD	American SB, Lorain	—	Cancelled Dec 1943
PF96	MACON	American SB, Lorain	—	Cancelled Dec 1943
PF97	LORAIN (ex-Sitka)	American SB, Lorain	—	Cancelled Dec 1943
PF98	VALLEJO	American SB, Lorain	—	Cancelled Dec 1943
PF99	ORLANDO	American SB, Cleveland	1.12.1943	Sold Nov 1947
PF100	RACINE	American SB, Cleveland	15.3.1944	Sold Dec 1947
PF101	GREENSBORO	American SB, Cleveland	9.3.1944	Sold Feb 1948
PF102	FORSYTH	American SB, Cleveland	20.5.1944	To Holland July 1947

These ships, modelled on the British 'River' class, were the Maritime Commission's attempt to reduce the shortage of ocean escorts. Its yards could not build to naval specifications; instead, the 'River', already adapted to mercantile standards, was further adapted to US prefabricated building methods and the British powerplant replaced by a US-type triple expansion reciprocating engine. The result, although externally quite similar to the destroyer escort, was considered decidedly inferior. It had a much larger turning circle, and its hull structure showed many more discontinuities and hence was considered far weaker, particularly in the face of underwater explosions. The frigates were also criticised as very hot below decks, perhaps due to their British design origin, with its emphasis on North Atlantic operations.

Two 'Rivers' were obtained from Canada to serve as prototypes; they became PF1 and 2 in a new series. Another hundred were ordered from the Maritime Commission; four were cancelled (PF95–98). PF72–92 were transferred to the Royal Navy, which named them after British colonies; the remainder were manned by the US Coast Guard. PF17, 18, 20, 23, 24, 28–33, 40, 41, 66–69, 71, 93, 94 and 99–102 operated as weather ships, with a balloon hangar replacing the after 3in/50 gun. Many were transferred to other navies in this form, and operated postwar as part of the international North Atlantic weather organisation. In addition, *Asheville* (PF1) served as trials ship for Squid, which the US Navy was considering for adoption, in 1944.

In 1945, 28 units were transferred to the Soviet fleet. When returned these were laid up in Japan, but at the outbreak of the Korean War they were recommissioned for the US and Korean navies; others went to Japan. All other frigates were discarded at the end of the war, as they were inferior to the destroyer escorts in everything but cruising endurance.

Launched 1943 and transferred on loan in 1953. They are named after trees, as were IJN destroyers. *Keyaki* had a deckhouse added abaft the mainmast and served as a flotilla flagship; *Kaede* received a similar deckhouse. All ships were technically returned on 28.8.62, but were immediately transferred outright to the Japanese government the same day. *Kusu* was converted to a drone target carrier in 1964. The following units were reclassified from escort vessels to training ships (moored): *Buna* (1.2.65), *Kashi* (1.4.65), *Momi* (1.4.65), *Tochi* (1.4.65), *Ume* (1.4.65), *Kaede* (31.3.66), *Maki* (31.3.66), *Matsu* (31.3.66), *Nara* (31.3.66), *Sakura* (31.3.66). *Tsuge* was discarded in 1968; *Nire* and *Shii* were returned to the USA on 31.3.70; and *Kiri*, *Keyaki* and *Sugi* were decommissioned 31.3.70.

Ex-US TACOMA class *frigates*

Particulars: As US *Tacoma* class

No	Name	Builder	Acquired	Fate
PF 281	KUSU (ex-Ogden)	Consolidated, San Pedro	1953	Deleted 1972
PF 282	NARA (ex-Machias)	Froemming	1953	Deleted 1972
PF 283	KASHI (ex-Pasco)	Kaiser, Richmond	1953	Deleted 1972
PF 284	MOMI (ex-Poughkeepsie)	Butler	1953	Deleted 1972
PF 285	SUGI (ex-Coronado)	Consolidated, San Pedro	Jan 53	Decommissioned 31.3.70
PF 286	MATSU (ex-Bath)	Froemming	Dec 53	Deleted 1972
PF 287	NIRE (ex-Sandusky)	Froemming	1953	Returned 31.3.70
PF 288	KAYA (ex-San Pedro)	Consolidated, San Pedro	1953	Deleted 1972
PF 289	UME (ex-Allentown)	Froemming	Apr 53	Deleted 1972
PF 290	SAKURA (ex-Carson City)	Consolidated, San Pedro	Apr 53	Deleted 1972
PF 291	KIRI (ex-Everett)	Kaiser, Richmond	Mar 53	Decommissioned 31.3.70
PF 292	TSUGE (ex-Gloucester)	Butler	1953	Deleted 1958
PF 293	KAEDE (ex-Newport)	Butler	1953	HS 31.3.68
PF 294	BUNA (ex-Bayonne)	American SB	1953	Deleted 1972
PF 295	KEYAKI (ex-Evansville)	Letham D Smith	Oct 53	Decommissioned 31.3.70
PF 296	TOCHI (ex-Albuquerque)	Kaiser, Richmond	1953	Deleted 1972
PF 297	SHII (ex-Long Beach)	Consolidated, San Pedro	1953	Returned 31.3.70
PF 298	MAKI (ex-Charlottesville)	Butler	Jan 53	Deleted 1972

Tacoma-class Frigate --- General Plans

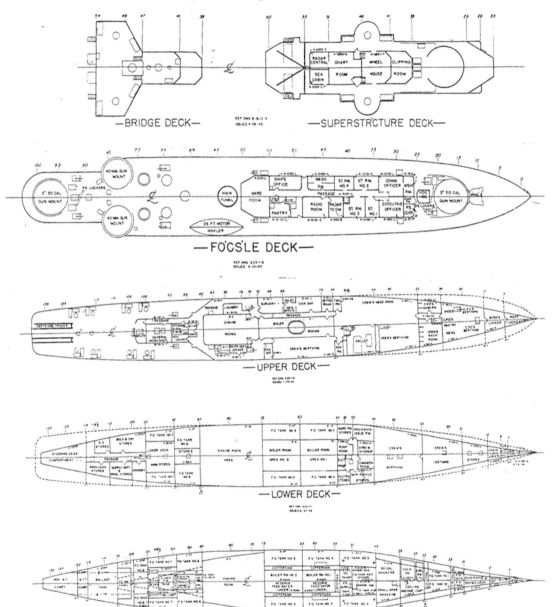

—BRIDGE DECK—

—SUPERSTRUCTURE DECK—

—FO'C'SLE DECK—

—UPPER DECK—

—LOWER DECK—

—HOLD—

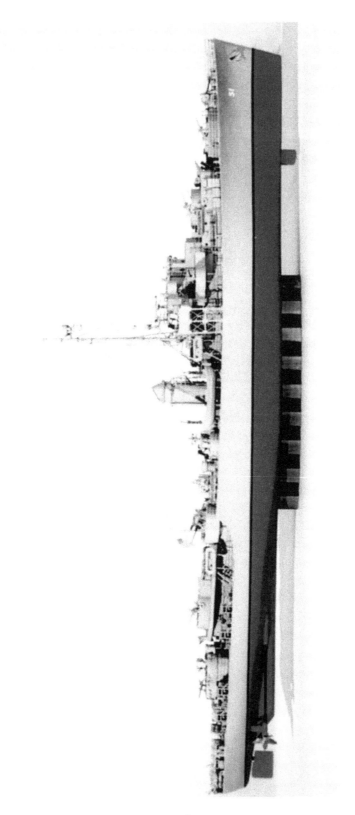

USS *Burlington* (PF-51), scale of model 1/8" = 1' --- built by Richard W. Ross

CHAPTER 1

A Review

The seventy-five Coast Guard-manned patrol frigates of World War II deserve a place in memory, if for no other reason than that they were the Navy's first line of combat vessels designated as frigates since the age of sail. The *Oliver Hazard* Perry-class of Cold War frigates gave birth to the term once again in the 1960s; however, in the years immediately following World War II, the mere mention of wartime service aboard a frigate would inevitably invite quips about the likes of *"Old Ironsides"* sailing into battle rigged with masts and sails, just about what the Coast Guard was accustomed to, some would add. Not forgotten by patrol frigate sailors, the frigates as a class won their share of battle stars. From the bitter cold of the northern reaches of the Atlantic, to warding off of kamikaze attacks on the road to Leyte, not one PF was lost during the war. Attesting to the seamanship and combat readiness of the Coast Guard officers and men, the PFs were the only American warship class of large numbers to boast this unique distinction. From early 1944 to war's end, ships of the "Forgotten Fleet" performed a full range of vital assignments in every major water body on earth, be it weather patrol operating in the icy chill out of Argentia, Newfoundland, to the tropics of Recife, Brazil, or escort duty from Norfolk across the Atlantic to Oran in the Mediterranean, or 'ping patrol,' convoy and invasion screening from New Guinea to Leyte Gulf, or guard ship station patrol off the Russian Komandorski Islands in the Bering Sea.

Apart from the heroics and call to duty aboard the frigates, once approved for construction in December 1942, the building and outfitting program suffered discouraging delays. As an antisubmarine craft for the Battle of the Atlantic, the program was hopelessly lost since the first frigates did not go to sea until January 1944, long after the U-boat menace was on the wane, and in any case, the success of the destroyer escort as the all-purpose antisubmarine and escort vessel made certain that the frigates would be assigned a host of alternative tasks. By mid-1942, authorized naval shipyards from Massachusetts to Mare Island in California had DEs on the ways, so that by the time the PFs were approved there was no room at the inn. Destroyer escorts were built in greater numbers than any other class of warships, 200 were at sea by early 1943, more than 500 by 1944, and mad-paced construction ended only when 305 contracts were cancelled in late 1943 to make way for invasion landing craft, mainly the LST and LCI. Seventy-eight DEs were delivered to Britain as Captain-class frigates, affectionately known as "Yankee Frigates" in the Royal Navy.

As planning progressed on what would become the patrol frigate program, C.N.O. Admiral Ernest King recommended merchant shipyards on the Great Lakes in the belief that the new construction would likely be corvettes, a vessel of established construction in Canada, 111 built for the RCN and 11 for the USN by 1943. The 205 foot, single screw, 16 knot *Flower* class corvettes, designed as coastal escorts were early pressed into Atlantic duty, earning their reputation as one of the wettest and uncomfortable warships afloat, but just the type of ship that the Coast Guard could live with, grumbled some old cutter men. Fortunately, once the Battle of the Atlantic took shape in 1940, the Royal Navy realized that the "Flowers" would not be big or fast enough for arduous deep-water service. The Admiralty moved fast toward a larger class of escort referred to during initial construction as 'twin screw corvettes: then officially defined as *River-class* frigates as the program moved ahead. All this brings to mind the classic British wartime film "The Cruel Sea" in which actor Jack Hawkins, skipper of a "Flower," after months of heavy weather battering on the corvette earned the good fortune of command of the new *River-class* frigate *Saltash.* In the film, however, *Saltash* was in fact a *Castle-class* corvette, the ultimate in RN corvette design. Fifty-seven "Rivers" slipped down the ways by late 1942, quickly called to the attention of the American Navy, partly because of their similarity to the DEs in size, speed and armament. Upon Admiral King's recommendation, following naval architects Gibbs and Cox redesign of the British frigate as an all-welded vessel subject to prefabrication and mass production, President Roosevelt ordered the Maritime Commission to award sixty nine contracts to merchant shipyards in December 1942. Earlier, two Canadian built prototypes, *Asheville* (PF-1) and *Natchez* (PF-2), were turned over to the U.S. Navy in "reverse lend-lease." Both ships retained a profile similar to the British *River-class,* namely in the squared off bridge and wheelhouse with no porthole windows as opposed to the *Tacoma-class* with rounded wheelhouse circled by seven porthole windows. Patrol frigate orders were soon increased to 100, four later cancelled and twenty-one approved for construction at the new Walsh-Kaiser yard in Providence, Rhode Island, for transfer to the Royal Navy under Lend Lease.

Apparently, the new Providence yard escaped the delay problems soon to plague the Great lakes yards, since launchings stormed ahead with all twenty-one afloat by November 1943. The Royal Navy proclaimed the speed of building phenomenal as the Union Jack was run up at Walsh-Kaiser on the new *Colony-class* frigates. In home waters the American made all welded frigates claimed six U-boats by war's end, the first by HMS *Ascension* on 25 November 1944, and the last by HMS *Anguilla* on 29 April 1945. Late in the European war HMS *Caicos* was converted to a Fighter Direction Ship and anchored in the North Sea off Harwich to warn of approaching V1 flying bombs and V2 rockets being fired against the UK from Holland. Late in 1944, with plans underway for transfer of a large number of RN escorts to the Pacific theater, it was argued that most of the Colony-class should be converted to Fighter Direction Ships to give some measure of aircraft protection to convoys not covered by aircraft carriers.

FRIGATES (Ex-American)

Colony class

Displacement: 1.318 tons.
Dimensions: 285½ (pp) 304 (oa) × 37½ × 12 ft.
Machinery: 2-shaft Reciprocating (V.T.E.), I.H.P. 5,500 = 18 knots.
Armament: 3—3 in. A.A. (3 × 1), 4—40 mm. A.A. (2 × 2), 4—20 mm. A.A. (4 × 1) guns.
Complement: 120.

K.500	ANGUILLA (ex-Hallowel, ex-PF.72)	Walsh Kaiser	14. 7.43	Returned U.S.N. 1946.
K.501	ANTIGUA (ex-Hammond, ex-PF.73)	,,	26. 7.43	Returned U.S.N. 1946.
K.502	ASCENSION (ex-Hargood, ex-PF.74)	,,	6. 8.43	Returned U.S.N. 3/46.
K.503	BAHAMAS (ex-Hotham, ex-PF.75)	,,	17. 8.43	Returned U.S.N. 1946.
K.504	BARBADOS (ex-Halsted, ex-PF.76)	,,	27. 8.43	Returned U.S.N. 13/4/46.
K.505	CAICOS (ex-Hannam, ex-PF.77)	,,	6. 9.43	Argentinian SANTIS-IMA TRINIDAD (1947), TRINIDAD (1947).
K.506	CAYMAN (ex-Harland, ex-PF.78)	,,	22. 8.43	Returned U.S.N. 22/4/46.
K.507	DOMINICA (ex-Harnam, ex-PF.79)	,,	14. 9.43	Returned U.S.N. 4/46.
K.584	LABUAN (ex-Gold Coast, ex-Harvey, ex-PF.80)	Walsh Kaiser	21. 9.43	Returned U.S.N. 5/46.
K.585	TOBAGO (ex-Hong Kong, ex-Holmes, ex-PF.81)	,,	17. 8.43	Returned U.S.N. 5/46; Egyptian (1950) but conversion from mercantile abandoned 1956 and scrapped.
K.586	MONTSERRAT (ex-Hornby, ex-PF.82)	,,	28. 8.43	Returned U.S.N. 6/46.
K.587	NYASALAND (ex-Hoste, ex-PF.83)	,,		Returned U.S.N. 4/46.
K.588	PAPUA (ex-Howett, ex-PF.84)	,,	10.10.43	Returned U.S.N. 5/46; Egyptian (1950) but conversion from mercantile abandoned 1956 and scrapped.
K.589	PITCAIRN (ex-Pilford, ex-PF.85)	,,	15.10.43	Returned U.S.N. 6/46.
K.590	St. HELENA (ex-Pasley, ex-PF.86)	,,	20.10.43	Returned U.S.N. 4/46.
K.591	SARAWAK (ex-Patton, ex-PF.87)	,,	25.10.43	Returned U.S.N. 5/46.
K.592	SEYCHELLES (ex-Pearl, ex-PF.88)	,,	30.10.43	Returned U.S.N. 6/46.
K.593	PERIM (ex-Sierra Leone, ex-Phillimore, ex-PF.89)	,,	5.11.43	Returned U.S.N. 5/46.
K.594	SOMALILAND (ex-Popham, ex-PF.90)	,,	11.11.43	Returned U.S.N. 5/46.
K.595	TORTOLA (ex-Peyton, ex-PF.91)	,,	16.11.43	Returned U.S.N. 5/46.
K.596	ZANZIBAR (ex-Prowse, ex-PF.92)	,,	21.11.43	Returned U.S.N. 5/46.

Colony-class frigate HMS *Caicos* (ex PF-77) at Harwich on the North Sea, April 1945. Her role at anchor as a Fighter Direction Ship.

Royal Navy *River*-class frigate HMS *Tay* as she appeared in early 1945. Note the similarity to the *Tacoma*-class patrol frigates.

David Hendrickson

The U.S. Navy's first modern "frigate," the Canadian-built USS Asheville (PF-1). Official USN Photograph (National Archives) 80-G-71285. This view was taken at 1200 on 12 June 1943 by ENS J. O. Barbour USN aboard blimp ZNP K-28 at an altitude of 200 ft. using a K-20 camera. At this time, Asheville was located in position 35 deg. 55'N, 73 deg, 51'W, underway at 12 knots escorting convoy NG 367 a day out from New York en route to Guantanamo Bay, Cuba.

However, upon careful consideration it was decided that inadequate ventilation below decks made these ships less than ideal for Pacific and East Indies service, a fact that somehow was lost on the U.S. Navy as eighteen *Tacoma-class* patrol frigates built by Consolidated Steel of Wilmington/San Pedro departed California, beginning in January 1944, assigned to the Seventh Fleet amphibious division in New Guinea waters. From New Caledonia to Leyte, frigate sailors complained bitterly of inadequate ventilation that generated stifling conditions below decks. All twenty-one *Colony-class* frigates were returned to the USN in 1946, laid up on the Potomac River and later scrapped.

On the drawing boards the new American fighting ships were initially classed as gunboats (PG) to be named for small cities in keeping with the 1933 *Eire-class* gunboat and her sister, *Charleston.* But since the American design so closely resembled the British version, designation was changed to frigate (PF) in mid-April 1943, the P to identify a patrol-type

5

vessel, not to be confused with the DEs where D designated a destroyer-type combat vessel. Beyond that, size, speed and armament of the two were surprisingly similar. The frigates displaced 1430 tons, were 303'11" in length, 37'6" in breadth, draft 13'8." Twin screws kicked up a foaming wake powered by triple expansion reciprocating steam engines capable of cranking out an acceptable 20.3 knots at flank speed. Limited to a single rudder and deeper draft by two feet, the frigates were no match for the twin rudder DEs in nimble maneuvering. On the other hand the deep draft and wide beam of the frigates provided noteworthy sea kindliness, and not the least, the high freeboard of the lengthy forecastle deck protected to a large degree against the threat of green water piling on board in heavy weather. The diesel powered DEs and steam powered PFs were near comparable in endurance, the DEs 10,800 nautical miles at 12 knots and the PFs 9,500 nautical miles at like speed. Nearly comparable in armament also, the frigates mounted 3-inch 50s, two forward and one aft, port and starboard midship twin-40mm Bofors and nine 20mm Oerlikons. Antisubmarine armament included a hedgehog forward (a 24 spigot mortar, Mk 10, firing an elliptical pattern over the bow, range 250 yds.) and depth charge racks and K-guns on the fantail. Complement of each frigate numbered 190 officers and men.

The frigate building program proceeded with all deliberate speed at the two California yards, Consolidated Steel Company of Wilmington/San Pedro and Kaiser Cargo Corporation at Richmond on San Francisco Bay. In both yards, keel-laying to commissioning averaged no more than seven months, and in the case of most of the eighteen Consolidated Steel ships, post-shakedown availability was of short duration so that *Long Beach, Glendale, Coronado* and San *Pedro* were on their way to the South Pacific as early as January and February 1944. Others followed in short order with the last, *Burlington,* on her way south in August. The case of the twelve Kaiser frigates was not quite so clean. Of PFs 3 to 8, only *Albuquerque* and *Everett* advanced on schedule to be on their way to long haul assignment in the Bering Sea by April *1944. Tacoma,* bearing the class name and the first launched at Richmond, plagued by unsuccessful sea trials, hot bearings and a boiler room fire, missed her Bering Sea assignment until coming in out of the cold at Adak on 21 October 1944. Likewise, *Sausalito, Hoquiam* and Pasco postponed arrival in the Aleutians until autumn 1944 because of protracted post shakedown availability. Kaiser frigates Nos. 9 to 14, following shakedown, were assigned to Western Sea Frontier operations out of San Diego, San Francisco and Seattle.

Six Great Lakes yards, two on far western Lake Superior, two on Lake Erie and two on the Wisconsin shore of Lake Michigan were awarded forty-nine frigate contracts. Four contracts held by American Shipbuilding of Lorain, Ohio, were cancelled before the program ended. Plagued by delays, Great Lakes built frigates averaged fourteen months from keel-laying to commissioning. *Bayonne* and *Alexandria* held the record at 21 months 8 days and 20 months 18 days respectfully. An early snafu appeared when Kaiser, responsible for materials, specifications and working drawings, designed prefabrication segments easily handled by Kaiser 50 ton load cranes, only to discover that cranes at the Great Lakes yard could lift no more than 10 tons. Once launched, each new frigate faced no less than a 2000 mile trip to salt water. Without a St. Lawrence Seaway to accommodate transit to Atlantic parts for outfitting, the Mississippi River was the only route to the sea. From the six yards the frigates were ferried to Chicago at the lower end of Lake Michigan. Then with pontoons fitted fore and aft, raising the draft to less than 9 feet, (9 feet was the standard constant waterway depth maintained by the Army Engineers), and the mast lowered to allow passage under bridges, each future combat vessel slipped into the Chicago Sanitary Ship Canal and on to the Illinois River waterway, through locks to reach the Mississippi above Alton, Illinois, through the Alton Locks and on to. St. Louis for the final 1000 mile run down the steamboat highway to the Gulf of Mexico. Some were outfitted in New Orleans and nearby Louisiana yards. Others had to navigate an additional 500 miles to Galveston and Houston in search of outfitting. Delays notwithstanding, a considerable number completed shakedown and reported for duty by mid-year 1944, some for Atlantic convey assignment, others converted for weather duty in the North Atlantic, and to the complete surprise of the eighteen California frigates attached to the amphibious division of the Seventh Fleet in the South Pacific, along came Great Lake boats *Sandusky*, *Machias*, *Allentown* and *Charlottesville* to horn in and join the party.

Beginning in mid-1943, the Coast Guard was faced with organizing manning sections to provide nearly 15,000 officers and men for seventy-five frigates. To meet the challenge, shore billets were eliminated, beach patrol units closed down and schools for all ratings expanded on training stations such as Manhattan Beach, New York, and Government Island, California. By spring 1944 only the lagging commissioning schedules of the Great Lakes PFs kept eager crews from boarding. For instance, in May 1944, twenty-six crews had completed training and were awaiting call at Manhattan Beach, and some 3,000 men were in temporary quarters along the Gulf Coast, standing by as their ships were fitted out in scattered yards. The manning section on Government Island operated a well-oiled program of dispensing crews to frigates launched at Richmond and San Pedro. All west coast frigates completed shakedown exercises at San Diego, while Bermuda waters were the location of shakedown for frigates outfitted on the Gulf coast. By the end of 1944, no theater of war, no ocean, no major sea was unknown to the patrol frigates; from the North and South Atlantic to the North and South Pacific, from the Indian Ocean and the Tasman Sea to the Coral Sea and the Philippine Sea, from the Caribbean Sea to the Mediterranean Sea, from the Gulf of Alaska through Unimak Pass to the storm plagued Bering Sea. Their exploits and memories of their crewmen are the subject of following chapters.

With the end of the war in Europe on 8 May 1945, the role of escort vessels in the Atlantic was over; the ocean soon largely abandoned except for the twenty or more patrol frigate weather ships on station from the Arctic to the Equator. In the Pacific the Philippines had been secured, Iwo Jima was in American hands, Okinawa was in the cleanup stage and the home islands of Japan being pounded unmercifully by B-29s from the Marianas. Earlier in the year new DEs mounting 5-inch guns and capable of 24 knots replaced the Seventh Fleet frigates for duty elsewhere, six of which were sent to the Aleutians to join up with the five of Escort Division 27. A number of the others were sent home for conversion to weather ships. Clearly the PFs were no longer considered necessary to the closing days of the war. So it is not at all surprising that the Navy willingly approved of twenty-eight frigates, more than one-third of the Coast Guard manned fleet, for Lend-Lease to the USSR.

It all came about as a result of the Yalta Conference of February 1945. The United States secured Soviet promise of entry into the Pacific war by pledging military goods and support for Russian acquisition of the Japanese Kuril Islands that enclose the Sea of Okhotsk. So Navy Detachment 3294, known as Project Hula was born. Rapid preparation of Cold Bay near the tip of the Alaskan Peninsula was underway in March as the secret exchange base, Captain William Maxwell USN in command and Commander John Hutson USCG, executive officer. As early as January 1945, Admiral King had informed Admiral Frank Jack Fletcher, Commander, Alaska Sea Frontier, of his intention to transfer up to 250 naval vessels to the USSR during the period April to December 1945. Cold Bay was chosen over Dutch Harbor and Kodiak because of remoteness and no nearby civilian population, a suitable Navy auxiliary air facility, a large anchorage in Kimzaroff Lagoon and protected waters for steaming and firing practice. Lastly, as one visitor put it, Cold Bay was safe from prying eyes since no one remembers having ever seen the sun break through the low overcast. The Navy Construction Battalion was called on to rehabilitate Fort Randall barracks and outbuildings. In no time and in "can do" fashion the Seabees set up Quonset huts for classrooms, built a radio station and several movie theaters and scooped out a softball field dubbed Yankee Stadium. Following discussions, the Russians agreed to transport sailors to Cold Bay aboard freighters returning empty to West Coast ports from Vladivostok for Lend-Lease goods, each ship scheduled to carry 600 men. So rapidly did events move along that the Soviets informed Captain Maxwell that 2,300 men would arrive by 1 April, 550 more by 1 May and 2,000 more by the 1st of June, Maxwell and Hutson had their work cut out in time and resources to train 15,000 Soviet naval personnel for a variety of American vessels, the first to arrive about the 1st of May. Shore based training at first was hampered by inadequate numbers of interpreters, almost non-existent Russian language manuals and the discovery that the Russian sailors knew almost nothing about radar, sonar and very little about engineering plants from diesel to steam. But American instructors reported that they were eager learners and once the Russian language manuals were in hand, training forged ahead to the point that when the Russian sailors went aboard ship, transfer for the smaller vessels took place in less than two weeks and less than one month for the frigates. From May to September 1945, 149 vessels were turned over to the Russians: frigates, minesweepers, LCI(L)s, subchasers and four floating workshops. The LCI(L)s were the first to haul down the flag and the frigates wound up the program in September. Vessels arrived manned by greatly reduced crews and further reduced as Russian sailors boarded and underway training proved successful. In terms of size, armament and value, the Tacoma-class frigates represented the most valuable vessels transferred at Cold Bay. Once the American flag was lowered and the Soviet ensign raised, the new Russian units departed quickly in groups for Petropovlovsk on Kamchatka Peninsula for assignment to the Soviet Far East Fleet.

Upon being relieved of duty in the South Pacific, Escort Division 25,*Long Beach, Coronado, San Pedro, Glendale, Belfast* and *Ogden,* in the first group of frigates loaned to the Soviets, made for Boston for overhaul and refit, arriving on 24 January 1945, Here according to the Lend-Lease agreement numerous alterations "changed the electrical equipment and armament to conform with the new allowance," CortDiv 25 got underway for Seattle via the Panama Canal on 28 March and then after final alterations slipped moorings for Kodiak on 7 June. Shortly after clearing Cape Flattery, *Ogden* had to break formation for return to Seattle to repair a salt water leak in a fresh water tank. The others steamed on to be joined in Kodiak by the four Great Lakes-built companions of the SW Pacific campaign: *Charlottesville, Machias, Sandusky* and *Allentown.* All nine got under way for the last leg on 13 June and dropped anchor in Kimzaroff Lagoon, Cold Bay, the next day. With fresh water tanks full, *Ogden* joined the crowd within days. The aboard ship training program began immediately, proceeding at the same pace for all. Using *Coronado* as an example, by late June the Russian engineering force was aboard as was the new CO and other officers. By 1 July, the entire Soviet crew of twelve officers and 178 men had embarked and by 7 July only four American officers and forty-four enlisted men remained for final days of training and decommissioning. From the bridge to the engine room, from the galley to the guns, *Coronado* was daily put through her paces in preparation for decommissioning day, 12 July 1945. At the appointed time Captain Maxwell and Rear Admiral Popov and their subordinates assembled on board *Coronado.* Transfer orders were read, a bugler played retreat, to hand salutes the U.S. flag came down and the Soviet colors run up. The Soviet crew took over. The last of the Americans marched off. Three days later, the first ten frigates, now numbered EK 1to 10 stood out of Cold Bay and in formation set course for Petropavlovsk. On 5 June, the last of CortDiv 27, *Albuquerque, Everett, Hoquiam* and *Sausalito,* departed the Aleutians for Seattle and refit, followed a month later by *Bisbee, Gallup, Rockford, Muskogee, Carson City* and *Burlington.* Joined later by *Tacoma* and *Pasco,* this crowd exchanged their PF numbers for EK numbers on 16 August and 26 August. To round out the twenty-eight frigates loaned to the Soviets, *Bayonne, Poughkeepsie, Gloucester, Newport, Bath* and *Evansville* hauled down the stars and stripes, the first two on 2 September (the day of Japanese surrender on board the *Missouri* in Tokyo Bay) and the last four on 4 September. The next day, 5 September 1945,

Captain Maxwell received the following dispatch:

ABSOLUTE STOP ON LEND LEASE DELIVERY ARMS AMMUNITION AND SHIPS HAS BEEN DIRECTED INCIDENT TO SURRENDER OF JAPAN X UPON RECEIPT OF THIS DESPATCH CEASE FURTHER DELIVERY OF VESSELS UNDER HULA AGREEMENT ...

Annapolis and *Bangor* steamed into Cold Bay on 12 September only to find that the party was over. Instead of taking on a Russian crew and making for Petropavlovsk, they took on board the last of the PF sailors beached in Cold Bay and acting as transports returned to Seattle. Admiral Popov and his staff and the last of the Russian trainees departed on 27 September on board the American Liberty ship *Carl Schurz.* As the month ended, Captain Maxwell closed his books, disposed of equipment, ordered his men sent home and decommissioned the base. In 142 days, Project Hula had transferred 149 ships to the Soviet navy. Four years elapsed before the Russians returned the frigates (October and November 1949) to the U.S. Navy in Yokosuka, Japan, all but *Belfast,* storm damaged and run aground in the Korsakov area off Sakhalin Island on 18 December 1948. The closing role and disposal of the Lend-Lease frigates to be told in a later chapter.

In the military might of nations, navies rank number one in unit costs. Thus once the fighting ends, ships are laid up. After Waterloo and the fall of Napoleon, Britain's fleet shrank by three-quarters, from a thousand ships in 1810 to three hundred in 1830. For much the same reasons of cost, following victory in World War II Halsey's Third Fleet was methodically broken up.

David Hendrickson

U.S. NAVY DETACHMENT 3294
COLD BAY, ALASKA
March 18 to September 11, 1945
Code Name HULA 2 (declasified)

This special Naval Detachment was established for the sole purpose of training Russian Naval Personnel to take over a number of U. S. Navy ships on the Lend Lease Program as established by the U.S. Congress. The Russians needed ships to stop the Japanese advancement along the Russian coast and Alaska.

Cold Bay, located at the end of the Alaskan Pen., was an ideal location, being a reasonable distance from Russian ports and Alaska. It was a deep water port with easy access to the sea and docking facilities and a warehouse which had been used by the Old Fort Randall. Another attribute was one of the best air strips in Alaska operated by the CAA.

The Navy took over the whole area, rehabilitated all of the housing and set up a training station, using a detachment of Seabees. The station was placed in commission on on March 20. 1945, when Capt. W. S. Maxwell USN arrived and took over command.

CDR. John J. Hutson. Jr. USCG was second in command and was designated Senior Training Officer. A shore based training program was set up using the US and USSR training officers. All of the training manuals had to be translated into Russian plus the various signs aboard each ship. A tremendous job which was accomplished in record time. The Russian staff turned out to be hard workers who got along very well with our US staff. The only real problems seemed to be language problems.

The training program was divided into a shore based training and on board training sessions. Class room studies using ship's manuals and the ASW class room work using installed equipment. Ship board training consisted of familiazation with the ship and on board equipment plus underway training . All guns were fired and all underwater sound (Sonar) and radar equipment tested. Naturally the engines were tested or we would not have had underway training.

Training was in phases, half of the American crew were replaced by Russians. then we kept dividing the crew until we had only key Americans left on board with a full Russian crew. At this point we conducted the transfer from the American flag to the Russian flag.followed by a big change of command party.

During the approximate 6 month period of training and transfer over 19,000 RUSSIAN Naval personnel manned 149 U.S. Naval craft and sailed them back to Russia.

| 28 PF's | 24 AM's | 31 YM'S |
| 30 LCI (1) 's | 32 sc's | 4 yr's |

Prepared by;

John J. Hutson, Jr.   PF-35
Capt. USCG (Ret)
12-30-94

11

U.S. Navy Combatant Ships Transferred to the USSR Under Project HULA, May–September 1945

U.S.	Designations Soviet	Transfer Date	Disposition	U.S.	Designations Soviet	Transfer Date	Disposition
Charlottesville (PF 25)	EK-1	12 Jul.	1949-returned	Penetrate (AM 271)	T-280	"	1960-scrapped
Long Beach (PF 34)	EK-2	"	"	Peril (AM 272)	T-281	"	1960-scrapped
Belfast (PF 35)	EK-3	"	1960-scrapped	Admirable (AM 136)	T-331	19 Jul.	1958-stricken
Glendale (PF 36)	EK-6	"	1949-returned	Adopt (AM 137)	T-332	"	1960-stricken
San Pedro (PF 37)	EK-5	"	"	Astute (AM 148)	T-333	"	1960-scrapped
Coronado (PF 38)	EK-8	"	"	Augury (AM 149)	T-334	"	1960-scrapped
Ogden (PF 39)	EK-10	"	"	Barrier (AM 150)	T-335	"	1956-scrapped
Allentown (PF 52)	EK-9	"	"	Bombard (AM 151)	T-336	"	1963-stricken
Machias (PF 53)	EK-4	"	"	Bond (AM 152)	T-285	17 Aug.	1960-scrapped
Sandusky (PF 54)	EK-7	"	"	Candid (AM 154)	T-283	"	1958-stricken
Tacoma (PF 3)	EK-11	16 Aug.	"	Capable (AM 155)	T-339	"	1960-scrapped
Sausalito (PF 4)	EK-16	"	"	Captivate (AM 156)	T-338	"	"
Hoquiam (PF 5)	EK-13	"	"	Caravan (AM 157)	T-337	"	"
Pasco (PF 6)	EK-12	"	"	Caution (AM 158)	T-284	"	"
Albuquerque (PF 7)	EK-14	"	"				
Everett (PF 8)	EK-15	"	"	LCI(L) 584	DS-38	10 June	1956-stricken
Bisbee (PF 46)	EK-17	26 Aug.	"	LCI(L) 585	DS-45	"	1955-returned
Gallup (PF 47)	EK-22	"	"	LCI(L) 590	DS-34	"	"
Rockford (PF 48)	EK-18	"	"	LCI(L) 591	DS-35	"	1956-stricken
Muskogee (PF 49)	EK-19	"	"	LCI(L) 592	DS-39	"	"
Carson City (PF 50)	EK-20	"	"	LCI(L) 593	DS-31	"	"
Burlington (PF 51)	EK-21	"	"	LCI(L) 665	DS-36	"	1955-returned
Bayonne (PF 21)	EK-25	2 Sep.	"	LCI(L) 667	DS-40	"	"
Poughkeepsie (PF 26)	EK-27	"	"	LCI(L) 668	DS-41	"	1956-stricken
Gloucester (PF 22)	EK-26	9 Sep.	"	LCI(L) 675	DS-42	"	"
Newport (PF 27)	EK-28	"	"	LCI(L) 943	DS-43	"	1945-combat loss
Bath (PF 55)	EK-29	"	"	LCI(L) 949	DS-44	"	1955-returned
Evansville (PF 70)	EK-30	"	"	LCI(L) 950	DS-32	"	1956-stricken
				LCI(L) 586	DS-37	14 June	1956-scrapped
Fancy (AM 234)	T-272	21 May	1960-scrapped	LCI(L) 587	DS-33	"	1956-stricken
Marvel (AM 262)	T-274	"	"	LCI(L) 521	DS-8	29 Jul.	1955-returned
Measure (AM 263)	T-275	"	"	LCI(L) 522	DS-2	"	"
Method (AM 264)	T-276	"	"	LCI(L) 523	DS-3	"	"
Mirth (AM 265)	T-277	"	"	LCI(L) 524	DS-4	"	"
Nucleus (AM 268)	T-278	"	"	LCI(L) 525	DS-5	"	1945-combat loss
Rampart (AM 282)	T-282	"	"	LCI(L) 526	DS-46	"	1955-returned
Disdain (AM 222)	T-271	22 May	"	LCI(L) 527	DS-7(?)	"	"
Indicative (AM 250)	T-273	"	"	LCI(L) 551	DS-48	"	"
Palisade (AM 270)	T-279	"	1957-stricken	LCI(L) 554	DS-9	"	1945-combat loss

U.S. Designations	Soviet	Transfer Date	Disposition	U.S. Designations	Soviet	Transfer Date	Disposition
LCI(L) 557	DS-10	"	1955-returned	YMS 285	T-610	27 Aug.	1945-sunk
LCI(L) 666	DS-50	"	1956-scrapped	YMS 287	T-611	3 Sep.	1955-stricken*
LCI(L) 671	DS-47	"	1945-combat loss				
LCI(L) 672	DS-1	"	1945-combat loss	SC 537	BO-304	26 May	1954-mothballed
LCI(L) 945	DS-6	"	1955-returned	SC 646	BO-310(?)	"	1956-destroyed
LCI(L) 946	DS-49	"	"	SC 647	BO-308	"	1956-stricken
				SC 661	BO-303	"	1954-mothballed
YMS 143	T-522	17 May	1956-stricken	SC 674	BO-306	"	1956-scrapped
YMS 144	T-523	"	1946-scrapped	SC 687	BO-301	"	"
YMS 428	T-525	"	1956-stricken	SC 657	BO-307	5 June	1954-stricken
YMS 435	T-526	"	"	SC 660	BO-311	"	1956-stricken
YMS 145	T-524	22 May	1956-destroyed	SC 663	BO-318	"	1955-stricken
YMS 59	T-521	6 June	1956-stricken	SC 673	BO-316	"	"
YMS 38	T-593	19 Jul.	1955-scrapped	SC 713	BO-313	"	"
YMS 42	T-592	"	1955-stricken	SC 986	BO-305	"	1954-stricken
YMS 75	T-590	"	1956-destroyed	SC 1021	BO-312	"	1955-stricken
YMS 139	T-594	"	1955-scrapped	SC 1060	BO-317	"	"
YMS 178	T-588	"	1956-destroyed	SC 500	BO-319	10 June	1956-destroyed
YMS 184	T-595	"	1955-stricken	SC 634	BO-309	"	1955-stricken
YMS 216	T-596	"	"	SC 675	BO-314	"	1956-stricken
YMS 237	T-589	"	1956-stricken	SC 1295	BO-320	"	1960-destroyed
YMS 241	T-591	"	1956-destroyed	SC 1324	BO-315	"	1956-stricken
YMS 272	T-597	"	"	SC 685	BO-302	19 Jul.	1948-stricken
YMS 273	T-598	"	1956-stricken	SC 538	BO-321	17 Aug.	1956-stricken
YMS 295	T-599	"	1956-destroyed	SC 643	BO-322	"	"
YMS 260	T-527	2 Aug.	1956-stricken	SC 752	BO-325	"	1955-stricken
YMS 33	T-603	17 Aug.	1956-destroyed	SC 754	BO-324	"	"
YMS 85	T-604	"	"	SC 774	BO-323	"	1956-stricken
YMS 100	T-602	"	"	SC 997	BO-326	"	1956-scrapped
YMS 266	T-601	"	1956-stricken	SC 1007	BO-332	"	1960-destroyed
YMS 288	T-600	"	1956-destroyed	SC 1011	BO-327	"	1955-stricken
YMS 301	T-605	"	1955-stricken*	SC 1031	BO-328	"	1960-destroyed
YMS 88	T-608	27 Aug.	"	SC 1364	BO-331	"	1956-scrapped
YMS 180	T-609	"	"	SC 1365	BO-329	"	1955-stricken
YMS 135	T-606	"	"	SC 756	BO-335	2 Sep.	1956-destroyed
YMS 332	T-607	"	"				

* subsequently transferred to the Peoples Republic of China

Soviet Designations
EK (storozhevoi korabl)–escort vessel
T (tralshik)–minesweeper
DS (desantiye suda)–landing ship
BO (bolshiye okhotniki za povodnimi lodkami)–large hunters
  for submarines

U.S. Designations
PF–frigate
AM–minesweeper
LCI(L)–large infantry landing craft
YMS–motor minesweeper
SC–subchaser

Sources: Department of the Navy, *Ships Data: U.S. Naval Vessels*, vol. II, 1 January 1949 (NAVSHIPS 250-012) (Washington: Bureau of Ships, 1949); S. S. Berezhnoi, *Flot SSSR: Korabli i suda lendliza: Spravochnik* [The Soviet Navy: Lend Lease Ships and Vessels: A Reference] (St. Petersburg: "Belen," 1994).

OPERATION HULA

by Virgil Davis - USS MUSKOGEE (PF-49)

Between August 9, 1945 and August 26, 1945, when the USS Muskogee
(PF-49) was decommissioned at Cold Bay, Alaska, I was a part of
the training crew whose responsibility was the instruction of the
Russian crew assigned to sail her to the Soviet Union. One
interpreter was available for passing our instructions to the
Russian crew and limited time to teach these crews did little to
help them absorb our detailed instructions. Because of the
limited time, the fact that most of the Russians had been
soldiers, these training sessions became total fiascoes.

One particular incident I recall, was instructing the Russian
doctor and a medic, the procedure we used to operate the
autoclave, a piece of medical equipment used to sterilize medical
instruments, bandages and other materials used in first aid boxes
about the ship and in the sick bay itself. The instrument itself
is similar to an oven, except it is air tight, and the
sterilization process uses high pressure steam for a prolonged
period of time. The time arrived for my instructions to be given
to the Russian doctor, the medic, and the interpreter to relay my
instructions to the three men. I explained very carefully, the
correct procedure, the time needed to complete the process, where
to open and close five or six valves controlling the high
pressure steam used in the process.

Upon completing my instructions, I asked if they had any
questions before they went through the procedure. None were
asked, they didn't go through the procedure and turned away to
walk on down the passage way. I assumed they didn't use
sterilized medical equipment, they were more intelligent than I
was, and they were not interested. I am certain of one thing,
opening or closing some of those high pressure steam valves may
have sent the autoclave directly through the overhead and through
the deck just forward of one of the 40 millimeter guns on the
deck. The ship did make it to Vladivostok, was a part of the
Russian Navy for five years before being returned to American
custody in Yokosuka, Japan in 1950. I do have two witnesses who
verified there were no holes in the deck of the ship. Perhaps
they never used the autoclave or maybe they were lucky!

The following taken from "Cold Sea - Lonely Sea" by David Hendrickson is an account of the Lend-Lease transfer of USS *Albuquerque* (PF-7) at Cold Bay, Alaska, August 1945.

Standing into Cold Bay on a dull gray Saturday, 14 July 1945, we first took on fuel from the ancient oiler *Tippecanoe* (AO-21), then moved to the anchorage to await developments. We swung at anchor until a landing barge pulled alongside a week later to carry off forty men and forty packed seabags. Four officers and the surgeon detached the next day, the 22nd, the day we weighed anchor for dock mooring between *Everett* and *Pasco*. The moment had arrived to welcome aboard our new shipmates. At 0945 some sixty or seventy Russian sailors stashed their gear on *Albuquerque's* fantail, a rather scruffy lot by our standards, but pleasant enough as we stepped forward as instructed to shake hands. Next our master-at-arms led the new frigate sailors to the mess deck for assignment to the "Glory Hole" and to be told through the interpreter of sole use of the crew head. The remaining American crew bunked on the mess deck and shared the chief's head with the four remaining CPOs. With the new crew aboard, the three frigates set special sea detail for return to the anchorage, the order coming first in English followed by Russian, which was common practice from that point on.

The beginnings of friendly mingling and sign language was apparent at the noon meal. The Russians seemed to enjoy American food. Large photos of Roosevelt, Truman and Stalin posted on the mess deck inspired cries of "comrade!, comrade!" At division muster that afternoon American sailors met their counterparts for division duties whether on the bridge, at the guns, in the galley or deep in the engine room. I met as usual with the dozen or so left in 2nd Division. Relieved of deck duties, I did not meet a Russian assigned to the laundry that day.

The next morning, alone, I stood face to face with two Russian trainees at the laundry half-door, unable to exchange a word. 'Semper Paratus' I thought, as I motioned them into the cramped quarters and began pointing to valves and switches and making circular motions of an operating washer and dryer. Ingenuity and good will prevailed, encouraged by sign language and quick use of our first words, "yes, no" and "da, nyet." All obstacles surmounted, within days the laundry was operating smoothly enough to pass inspection by FDR himself. He would have been pleased with this low-level consumation of Lend-Lease.

The training program began most mornings after breakfast by weighing anchor and making for the open sea for a day of exercises. Under manual control (electronic fire control had been removed during refit) guns were fired and engine capabilities demonstrated from slow to flank speed. After anchorage and evening chow the mess deck would darken for an American film, always looked forward to by the Russians, and when the lights came on we would linger to exchange coins, ribbons, postcards, buttons and insignias and other bits of memorabilia. The Russians were particularly intrigued with wrist watches, fountain pens and shiny black shoes.

Late on Saturday the 28th of July, we moored four deep at the docks alongside *Everett*, *Tacoma* and *Sausalito*, the training period for all four rapidly drawing down. On the 3rd of August, following two days at sea, a list of names on the mess deck bulletin board signified packed seabags and departure at 1500 the next day. I was seventh on the list. With this detachment, a mere handful of Americans remained aboard PF-7, soon to become a Russian EK boat. Seabags tossed into an open truck and sailors crowded into a Navy bus, we rumbled off to the airstrip to board a four-motored Navy aircraft bound for Kodiak Naval Air Station, three hours flying time away. My last glimpse of USS *Albuquerque* (PF-7), my home for the past twenty months, was through a small porthole window from a bucket seat at about 1000 feet altitude just prior to the aircraft's climb into the overcast. Patrol frigates 3,4,5,6,7, and 8, late of Escort Division 27, all on the same day, 16 August 1945, hauled down the American colors and ran up the Soviet ensign.

Franklin County Historical Society
305 North Fourth
Pasco, WA 99301, USA

Dear Sir:

There are enclosed date of ship PF-6 "Pasco" activity. PF-6 build by Kizer Cargo Navy Shipyard, Richmond, CA and commissioned as a patrol frigate to the US Navy on 15 April,44.

PF-6 transferred to the Soviet Navy on 16 August,1945 and left Cold Bay, CA for Petropavlovsk-Kamchatsky on 26 August, 1945. PF-6 commissioned to the Pacific fleet of the USSR and entered to the list of combat units of WW11 (08/26-09/3/45).

Patrol frigate PF-6 renamed to escort frigate ЭК-12 by order #108 of commander of the 5th surface ship group 10/5/45.

Commanding-officers of ЭК-12:

1. Captain-lieutenant KNIGA Gerasim Semenovich had been appointed 08/2/45 by order # 0619 of commander -in-chief of Pacific fleet.

2. Captain-lieutenant MIRONOV Leonid Sergeevich,the Hero of the Soviet Union, had appointed 12/26/46 by order # 0506 of Minister of the Navy.

3. Captain-lieutenant NESTERETZ Vasily Eremovich had appointed 02/01/49 by order # 0119 of commander-in-chief of the USSR Navy.

The crew ЭК-12 consisted of 189 member. They had successful results during ЭК-12's missions at the Sea and in particular escorted convoys of cargoships from Vladivostok to Port-Artur (1947-1948). Alsow ЭК-12 took part at support operations by transportation 500 touns of equipment's and foods to land units of the Navy and more than 200 touns of oil to Ust-Kamchansk's fishe plant.

In all, ЭК-12 operated at the Sea 4077 miles in 1947 and 6835 miles in 1948.

Source: Datefile 1393, List 33, point 31, p.p. 161-162

Some members of ЭК-12 crew had awarded in a honor of combat achievments.

Order of the Great Patriotic War -
1. Commanding-officer captain-lieutenant KNIGA Gerasim Semenovich, 1906, ukranien, in service since1928.

ЭК-12 decommissioned from the USSR Navy by order # 0035 of the 7th Russian fleet Commander-in-chief 03/8/50 and transfered to the US Navy

----

EK-9, the ex-*Allentown* (PF 52), and *EK-2*, the ex-*Long Beach* (PF 34), at Maizuru, Japan, prior to their return to the U.S. Navy in October 1949. Both ships later served in the Japanese Maritime Self-Defense Force.

Russian State Central Photo and Film Archives, Moscow

EK-22, the ex-*Gallup* (PF 47), inboard of the Soviet Type 7 destroyer *Razyashchy*, probably at Petropavlovsk. The American-built ship arrived at Petropavlovsk on 5 September 1945, too late to participate in operations against Japan.

Russian State Central Photo and Film Archives, Moscow

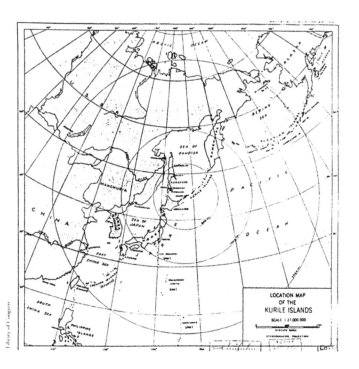

The map to the right shows the location of the Kuril Islands and the Aleutian Islands in relation to the Pacific. The close-up of the Aleutian Islands below shows the location of Cold Bay, in the upper right. The U.S. agreed to Soviet control of the Kuril Islands as a condition to that country's entry into the war against Japan.

Some ships laid up in the reserve fleet, others scrapped, and some sold off to emerging minor naval powers. The swift American demobilization reduced the Navy from 1,200 major combat vessels in 1945 to mere 267 by 1948. By July 1950 a nest of mothballed destroyers lined up in San Diego harbor numbered in excess of fifty.

The frigates were an easy target for rapid discard at war's end. As noted earlier, in excess of one-third of the fleet of seventy-five were subject to Lend-Lease, and of the remaining forty-seven, most were decommissioned by mid-1946, laid up awaiting the breakers or loaned or sold to deserving nations. A number of weather ships continued operations under the Coast Guard, but they too were gone by the end of 1946. Navy-manned *Ashville* and *Natchez* were sold to Argentina and the Dominican Republic in 1946 and 1947 respectively. *Eugene*, *Grand Island* and *Peoria* went to then friendly Cuba in 1947; *Eugene* renamed *Jose Marti* in remembrance of the anti-Spanish poet/revolutionary killed by the Spanish in 1895. *Grand Island* was renamed *Maxima Gomez* and *Peoria* became the *Antonio Maceo*, both leading insurgents in Spain's last days in Cuba in the 1890s. An additional twelve frigates laid up in early 1946 went to Latin American countries in 1947. Veteran weather ships *Muskegon*, *Emporia*, *Manitowoc* and *Lorain* went to France in 1947. Among those sold for scrap in 1947 were *Orlando*, *Orange*, *Davenport*, *Brownsville*, *El Paso*, *Corpus Christi*, *Grand Forks*, *Pocatello*, *Casper*, *Milledgeville*, *Moberly* and *Key West*. Two frigates still afloat by the turn of the century, both in service in the Royal Thai Navy, were *RTNS Tachin*, ex-*Glendale* and *RTNS Prasae* ex-*Gallup*.

It is fitting to close out Chapter 1 by recognizing the origin and history of the Patrol Frigate Reunion Association, founded in 1986 by two ex-crewmembers of *Grand Forks* (PF-11) and Roberta Shotwell, wife of deceased Chief Quartermaster Don Shotwell, Roberta soon assumed command of PFRA, continuing in firm leadership until her death in 2005, followed by a remembrance of her and breakup of PFRA in formal ceremony on Coast Guard Island, Alameda. 3 June 2005. Over the years PPRA met in annual reunions in cities from coast to coast.

At the San Francisco Peace Conference in late May 1945 that set in motion the creation of the United Nations, *Grand Forks* was chosen to welcome on board for a Bay tour and dinner, the distinguished United States representatives to the conference. On the evening of 31 May 1945 the official party led by Secretary of State Edward R. Stettinius Jr., and Mrs., Stettinius were greeted by commanding officer William F. Adams, the crew at quarters in dress blues and eight side boys at the gangway. In the party of nearly twenty were Senators Arthur Vandenberg of Michigan, Tom Connally of Texas, Nelson Rockefeller, Alger Hiss, Harold Stassen, and Assistant Secretary of State James Dunn.

Among major accomplishments of PFRA on the road to maturity are the following: honored as Coast Guard representative for the salute to the retiring carrier Hornet, 1995 at Alameda Naval Air Station; the placing of three monuments to the patrol frigates, the first at

Coast Guard Yard, Curtis Bay, Maryland, 25 May 1994; the second at Coast Guard Island. Alameda, California, 11 August 1994; and the last at Coast Guard Academy, New London, Connecticut. 6 September 1996.

10a

WWII Patrol Frigates Monument
Coast Guard Yard, Curtis Bay, Md.

CAPT George L. Sutton, USCGR(Ret.)

Patrol frigates were conceived as all-purpose gunships and their design was a refinement of the British "River Class" frigate. They were 308-feet long and performed convoy escort, anti-submarine warfare (ASW), shore support fire, anti-aircraft (AA) screen and ocean station duties in both the Atlantic and Pacific Theaters of Operation during World War II. Fifteen thousand Coast Guard personnel crewed 75 WWII patrol frigates. Patrol frigates were well-armed, with three three-inch 50-caliber deck guns, two twin-40 mm Bofors and eight single 20-mm Oerlikons for AA screen. ASW weapons included a Hedgehog mortar, eight depth charge throwers, two depth charge racks aft and a ram bow. Typical wartime crew size totalled about 200. Not one of them was lost during the war, attesting to the seamanship skills, leadership and combat readiness of the Coast Guard officers and men who sailed in them. In addition to the one shown here (yes, that's me pointing to the *USS Orange (PF-43)*, which I served aboard as a Watertender Fireman in 1945-46), there are two other monuments to the patrol frigates dedicated by the Patrol Frigate Reunion Association — one at Alameda, Calif. and another will be dedicated at the CG Academy on Sept. 6, 1996 by members of the PFRA during their annual reunion in Boston.

— *CAPT George L. Sutton, USCGR(Ret.)*
Roseland, N.J

The Coast Guard Reservist
May 1996

World War II Patrol Frigate Monument
Coast Guard Island, Alameda, Calif.

As a member of the Patrol Frigate Reunion Association (PFRA) and a plank owner of *USS Albuquerque PF-7*, I was one of the speakers at the Aug. 11, 1994 dedication ceremonies of the Patrol Frigate Monument located on Munro Circle at CG Island. The 75 Coast Guard-manned frigates of WWII are listed on the monument

David Hendrickson
Fresno, Calif.

David Hendrickson

The Coast Guard Reservist
June 1996

21

EAST COAST PATROL FRIGATE MONUMENT DEDICATED

George L Sutton, USS ORANGE PF-43

Several hundred guests attended the United States Coast Guard's World War II Anniversary commemoration on 25 April 1994 at the Coast Guard yard Curtis Bay, Maryland. The high point of the day for the many Patrol Frigate sailors present was the unveiling of a permanent monument dedicated to the memory of the World War II Patrol Frigate Coast Guard crews. The monument consists of an impressive bronze plaque mounted on a granite base located at the head of the Yard's parade ground. The plaque is dedicated to the Officers and men of the Coast Guard who manned these Patrol Frigates during World War II and lists the names of all 75 ships.

Special thanks go to Bill La Plante, USS Belfast (PF-35), for heading the Association's fund-raising effort and for bringing the monument to completion.

The Honor Guard for the dedication of the Memorial was William La Plant, USS Belfast (PF-35), Art Wells, USS Belfast (PF-35), Joe Gulick, USS El Paso (PF-41) and William Tyrrel, USS Gallup (PF-47).

The afternoon-long program also recognized the work done by CG Yard World War II civilian workers who built the CG Cutters Mendota and Pontchartrain, launched in 1943. The program also celebrated the 95th birthday of the CG Yard.

Each World War II Coast Guard veteran present received a Certificate of Appreciation signed by the Yard's Commanding Officer. Special honors were accorded the memory of the 1,038 Coast Guardsmen killed in World War II.

Featured speakers of the day were Radm Peter Bunch, Chief, Coast Guard HQ Office of Engineering, Capt R. J. Marafioti, Commanding Officer, CG Yard and Mrs. Roberta Shotwell, Chairman, Patrol Frigate Reunion Association.

Music was provided by the U. S. First Army Band and the USCG Academy Glee Club from New London, Connecticut, before, during and after the program.

On a personal note, seeing the name of my own ship permanently listed, along with all the other frigates on the memorial plaque, was a thrilling experience.

A reception and a tour of CG Yard exhibits set up in the Columbus Recreation Center followed the outdoor program.

If in the future, you are in the Baltimore area, don't miss the opportunity to visit the CG Yard and see the Patrol Frigate Memorial. The Yard is easy to reach from Route 695.

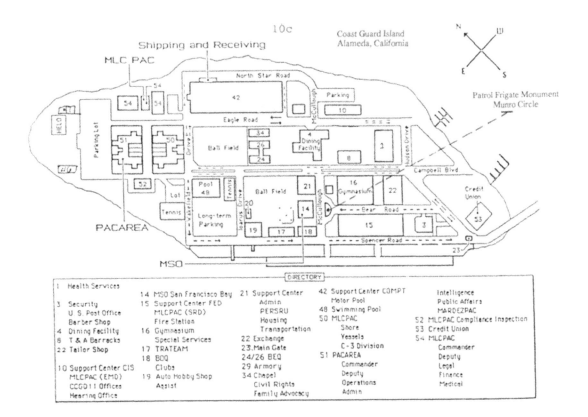

Patrol Frigate Monument
Coast Guard Island
Alameda, California
Dedicated 11 August 1994

10d

Dedication Ceremony - Memorial Monument
Coast Guard Island, Alameda, California, 11 August 1994

On a glorious cool and sunny day, 150 ancient mariners accompanied by wives and guests gathered at Munro Circle on Coast Guard Island at 1030 hours for the unveiling of a brass plaque commemorating the 75 Coast Guard-manned patrol frigates of WWII.

Following presentation of colors and invocation by Cmdr. Susan Garment USN, master of ceremonies, Cmdr. Manson Brown introduced our own Bobbie Shotwell, PFRA chairperson, for welcoming remarks. In brief historical reflections, Captain Sam Guill, skipper of USS Pocatello (PF-9), commented on weather duty on Station Able, North Pacific, followed by Dave Hendrickson, USS Albuquerque (PF-7), who described the role of the South Pacific and Bering Sea frigates. Bob DeWitt of USS Casper (PF-12), outlined the long campaign pursued by PFRA leaders and generous financial support of the membership that has resulted in locating patrol frigate memorials at Curtis Bay, Maryland, and here at Alameda. Bob closed with his poem in remembrance of 75 frigates and their gallant crews. Distinguished guests seated in the ceremonial front row were former Commandant, Admiral Chester Bender, Captain Christian Couser of USS Gloucester (PF-22) and Captain William Adams of USS Grand Forks (PF-11).

Preceding the unveiling, Rear Admiral Gordon G. Piché spoke movingly of the no longer "forgotten" patrol frigates. Above the three-column list of ship names on the unveiled brass plaque appeared the following declaration:

A "Well Done" to the officers and men
Of the United States Coast Guard
Who served aboard the Patrol Frigates
During World War Two
Their deeds are evidence of the best tradition
Of the United States Coast Guard
"SEMPER PARATUS"

Little did we know that under the granite block bearing the brass plaque, buried in time-lock plastic, lay the dog tags of Ed Mazzini of USS Hutchinson (PF-45). We understand that Ed slipped aboard Coast Guard Island to perform his honorable act just moments before the granite was set in place. Good show, Ed! Perhaps we can place 1000 more at a later date!

The day carried on with picnic lunch on the lawn adjacent to the dining facilities and tours of the island and visitation aboard 378 ft. USCGC Boutwell.

Ships represented at the ceremony were: Tacoma, Sausalito, Hoquiam, Pasco, Albuquerque, Pocatello, Brownsville, Grand Forks, Casper, Pueblo, Grand Island, Gloucester, Long Beach, Belfast, Glendale, San Pedro, Coronado, Ogden, Eugene, El Paso, Van Buren, Corpus Christi, Hutchinson, Bisbee, Gallup, Rockford, Muskogee, Burlington, Allentown, Sandusky, Monitowoc, New Bedford, Lorain, Milledgeville, Orlando.

Submitted by Dave Hendrickson

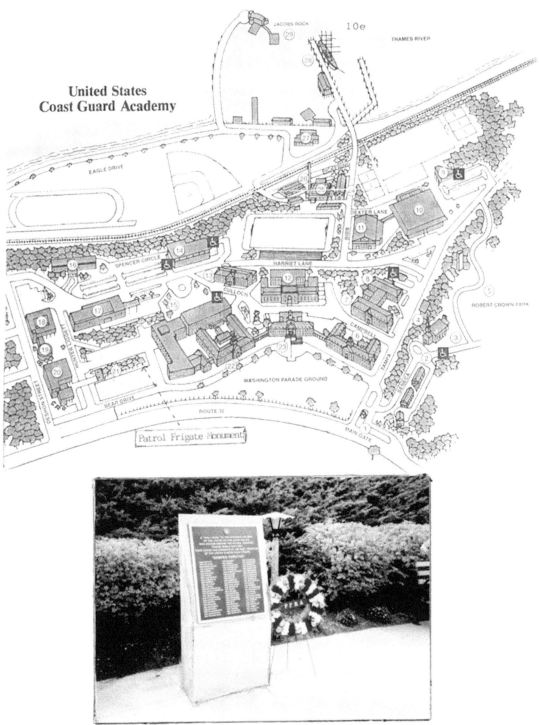

Patrol Frigate monument -- Coast Guard Academy
6 September 1996

10f

Dedication Day -- Patrol Frigate Monument
US Coast Guard Academy, New London Connecticut
6 September 1996

Our day at the Academy was best said by Louis Gamba, USS Ogden, PF-39:

This past reunion was the best ever. The highlight was our day at the Coast Guard Academy, the heart and soul of all of us. The ceremony, unveiling our bronze monument as the lone sailor sounded taps on her bugle, brought tears to our eyes. It was a nostalgic event, long to be remembered. Speeches by ex- Patrol Frigate sailors stirred old memories of battles fought in my youth. Cadets passing in review, the 60 piece band, precision marching and old glory flying in the breeze, were a fitting end to a one of a kind, never to be repeated day.

Our thanks to the following: Captain George Sutton PF-43 who memorialized the 75 Patrol Frigates and the duties performed by their crews; to Robert DeWitt PF-12, our resident poet, whose poem for the day touched our emotions; to Jim Matlock PF-38, who honored our departed as he placed a wreath at the base of the monument, and to Ed Burke PF-71, who participated in the unveiling of our PFRA monument.

The Honor Guard for the ceremony were the following:

Richard Leonis PF-42	Frank Intagliata PF-29
Mel Compton PF-41	Gerry Hoagland PF-39
William LaPlante PF-35	Louis Gamba PF-39
Art Wells PF-35	George Kupres PF-29
Ed Mazzini PF-45	Harry Nekonchuk PF-11
Doug Thornton PF-19	Jack Stewart PF-11

With the placement of this , our third and last monument, it completes a goal I set for the organization in 1992., to place three (3) monuments for the PFRA. The monument at Curtis Bay yard, was relatively easy, as they were having a celebration to honor the 50th Anniversary of the shipyard and two (2) ships. They agreed to a placement of a monument if it would be exactly like the existing Destroyer Escort one already there. We then used this at our other two (2) sites.

It took almost two (2) years to convince the base at Alameda, to accept our monument and then another two (2) years for the Coast Guard Academy to give permission to our group. I'm very grateful to Commander Manson Brown and the personnel at these installations who helped me obtain permission to place our legacies. We would like to express our thanks and gratitude to William LaPlante who tirelessly collected monies, ordered the monuments and plaques and made sure they arrived on time to be placed for ceremonies. (Bill only lost the Alameda one, but it was found in Arizona and delivered on time).

Roberta Shotwell, Chairman PFRA
Bobbie Freitas, Yeoman

CHAPTER 2

Tales of the Southwest Pacific

Twenty-one frigates participated in General MacArthur's New Guinea campaign and returned to the Philippines in 1944. These included all Consolidated Steel built-frigates, Nos. 34 to 51, except for *Corpus Christi* (PF-44) that steamed on by the jumping off points of Noumea, New Caledonia and Caims, Australia, where her sisters were enlisting one by one in Admiral Daniel Barbey's Seventh Fleet amphibious division. PF-44 continued on around the southern coast of Australia to Fremantle, the port for Perth, for a lengthy tour of submarine training exercises and lonely patrol in the Indian Ocean. All alone on 13 February 1945, she rescued ninety-two survivors of the torpedoed Liberty ship *Peter Sylvester.* On another patrol *Corpus Christi* was commended for refueling the British battleship *HMS Howe.* Joined by *Hutchinson* from Leyte in December 1944, these two set the frigate record for continuous time away from the States at sixteen months, returning to California in October 1945. Escorting six British transports bound for New Guinea, New Hebrides and the Solomons, four Great Lakes built frigates, *Allentown, Charlottesville, Machias* and *Sandusky,* arrived in New Guinea from Norfolk in September1944. Now the list was complete; twenty-one patrol frigates wed to the Seventh Fleet for operations stretching from the tail of bird-shaped New Guinea at Milne Bay to Leyte in the Philippines 2,000 miles northwestward. From the bird's tail at Milne Bay to the last stop in New Guinea at Cape Sansapor on the bird's head on Vogelkop Peninsula, familiar names to the frigate sailors included Cape Cretin, Saidor, Aitape, Hollandia, Wakde, Matlin Bay, Biak, Noemfoor, *and* Seeadler Harbor in the nearby Admiralty Islands. From New Guinea MacArthur's scheme drew the frigates northwest to Morotai in the Halmahera Islands, and lastly 500 miles farther on to 10 degree North Latitude for landings at Leyte. Through it all, the call to duty saw the frigate sailors through long and boring spells of antisubmarine patrol ('ping patrol'), sleepless invasion screening, plodding escort duty to and fro across the Equator from Hollandia 1,200 miles northwest to Leyte, occasional bombardment assignments and too often days on end at general quarters warding off air attacks in Leyte Gulf and San Pedro Bay, all endured on ships lacking suitable ventilation below decks. In the end, collectively, they were awarded fifty two battle stars as follows:

Glendale 5	*San Pedro 4*	*Coronado 4*
Long Beach 3	*El Paso 3*	*Ogden 3*
Van Buren 3	*Muskogee 1*	*Orange 2*
Eugene 2	*Belfast 2*	*Bisbee 2*
Burlington 2	*Carson City 2*	*Hutchinson 2*
Gallup 2	*Rockford 2*	*Charlottesville 2*
Allentown 2	*Machias 2*	*Sandusky 2*

Source: Dictionary of AMERICAN NAVAL FIGHTING SHIPS, 8 Vols.

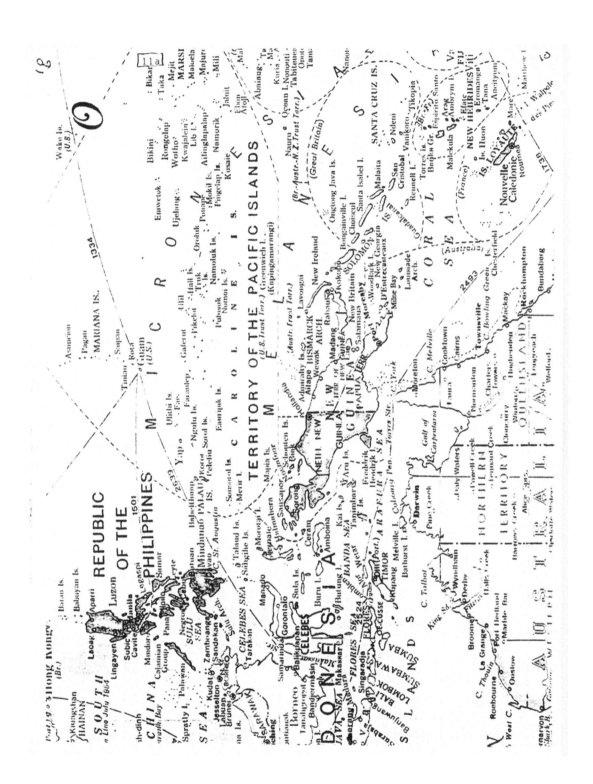

11b

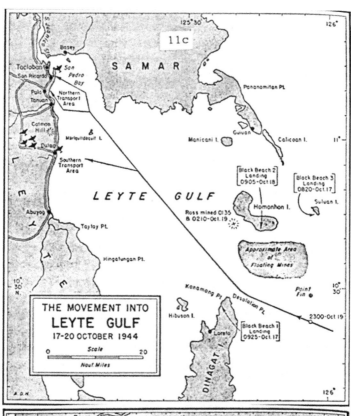

11c

THE MOVEMENT INTO
LEYTE GULF
17-20 OCTOBER 1944

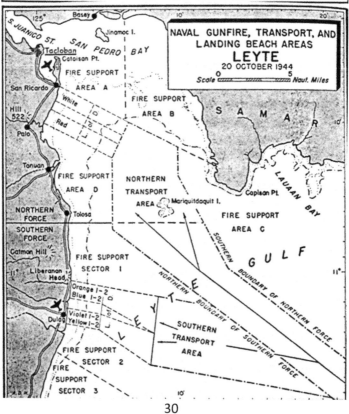

NAVAL GUNFIRE, TRANSPORT, AND
LANDING BEACH AREAS
LEYTE
20 OCTOBER 1944

200 miles off the New Guinea coast, at the head of the Bismarck Sea, lay the mountainous Admiralty Islands. Here, the Japanese had airfields on the two largest islands, Manus and Los Negros. Enclosed by islands on the northern fringe was Seeadler Harbor, large enough for fleet anchorage. By capturing the Admiralties, Japanese forces in the Bismarcks could be sealed off from reinforcements from the north, and a strategic location would be in Allied hands. An attack force under Rear Admiral W.M. Fechteler arrived off Los Negros on 29 February, and after bombardment, landings were affected. The islands were declared secured on 3 April with Japanese losses numbered at 2,600. Seeadler Harbor quickly became an important Allied air and naval base. During the campaign, *Coronado, Glendale, Long Beach* and *San Pedro* took part at various times as escorts for reinforcements and supplies and ASW screening on the perimeter of the Admiralties.

By late spring 1944, the re-conquest of New Guinea had gobbled up the eastern half of the 1,500 mile-long coastline. MacArthur then decided to push far to the northwest and seize Hollandia on Humboldt Bay and adjacent coastal points. Admiral Barbey, in overall naval command, chose a three force operation, one to land at Tanahmerah Bay to the west, the central group to strike at Humboldt Bay and the eastern force to take Aitape. The three groups comprised a total of 161 vessels, backed up by a reinforcement group of 50 ships. New arrivals from California, *El Paso, Ogden* and *Van Buren* joined the original four, *Coronado, Long Beach, Glendale* and San *Pedro* in the reinforcement group, all of which took turns at antisubmarine screening and one or more occasionally joined in bombardment.

Following air and naval bombardment, simultaneous surprise landings occurred and beachheads established at all points against virtually no opposition from the Japanese, most of whom fled into the mountainous interior. From the established beachheads, troops moved inland overcoming resistance and isolating the few remaining enemy to forgotten pockets from which they ultimately surrendered, were captured or died. United States losses in the campaign, when declared closed on 6 June, were less than 1,000 killed to the Japanese sacrifice of 14,000.

With the New Guinea campaign moving along at breakneck speed, accompanied by the fast task forces of the Central Pacific moving ever westward through Micronesia, MacArthur determined to grab off the bird's head of New Guinea and perhaps shorten the time for return to his beloved Philippines. On 17 May his forces stormed on 125 miles west of Hollandia to capture Wakde airfield and set the stage for Navy and Coast Guard-manned LSTs to assault Wakde Island, escorted and screened by frigates *El Paso, Ogden* and *Van Buren*. Soon it was time to take Biak, Noemfoor and the top of the bird's head at Cape Sansapor. Into the mix for these summer campaigns steamed another gang of frigates from California - namely, *Belfast, Hutchinson, Orange, Eugene, Gallup, Muskogee* and *Bisbee,* all quickly wise to the routine of 'ping patrol,' invasion screening and the monotony of escort duty. The Sansapor campaign was effectively over by the end of July. The Seabees landed and airfields were immediately under construction, bringing Celebes and Borneo into bombing range and affording land based bombers control over Japan's routes to the East Indies through the Straits of Makassar and the Molucca Sea. For weeks on end the frigates operated with little relief from mission to mission, seldom knowing what tomorrow would bring. An example of a quickly determined mission is described in an essay by Gordon Crawford of the *San Pedro*. Here edited for length.

> . .. Some of the troops fighting at Sarmi were taken away for the Biak invasion and the new battle was on. Biak's jungles and the enemy's determination not to give up made this a risky, costly light.
>
> As the *San Pedro* patrolled offshore from the beachhead, it was evident that the invasion was not going well for our assault forces. DUKWs churned past on their missions of mercy, delivering the dead and wounded to the hospital ship only a short distance from the San *Pedro.* From this very bloody and stalemated condition on the beachhead, it was determined by the big brass of the invasion forces that San *Pedro* would steam to the backside of Biak Island, in the area of Bosnik and Rani Island, and proceed to bombard the Japanese positions, which included their main supply base.
>
> On the morning of July 31, 1944, Brigadier General Doe, Brigadier General Zundel, a Dutch Lt. Colonel, and several native scouts, came aboard as observers. This turned out to be a very astute move, as the native scouts knew the exact location of the Jap supply bases. San *Pedro* commenced bombardment and soon had the supply bases on fire and in ruins. The Dutch officer remarked afterward that he had never witnessed such accurate firing... Our motor-whale boat and heavily-armed crew proceeded ashore to assess the results. They returned accompanied by Biak islanders in their native outrigger canoes and 25 Japanese soldiers who gladly surrendered to the *San Pedro* crew. These were some of the first Japanese prisoners of war in the Southwest Pacific. More Biak islanders came out with palm leaves filled with freshly-severed Japanese ears, that crewmen might have some souvenirs.... At Bosnik the prisoners of war departed in company of armed guards ... The *San Pedro* then got underway, standing out to assume antisubmarine patrol off-shore Biak...

Other Japanese prisoners were collected by frigate crews. *Coronado,* which had earlier off Aitape saved seven airmen from a ditched B-24, was on her way to antisubmarine patrol off Wadke on 5 June, when a crude raft was sighted bearing six men, who proved to be badly emaciated Japanese. They were picked up and turned over to PT-160 which delivered them to Wadke. On 27 July *Orange* was directed to embark three Army officers of a scouting party operating behind enemy lines near Sarmi Point west of Hollandia. The frigate groped its way around the point and, with all guns manned, closed the shore and dispatched her whaleboat with a landing party. The boat was met by a raft containing the scout group and two Japanese captives. Following the Leyte invasion *Allentown* made a brief visit to Morotai. Ashore, crewmen were approached by several Filipinos who explained that a Japanese soldier was hiding in the woods. A quickly organized search revealed the subject hiding behind a tree. Taken into custody, the now suspected spy was found to speak exceptionally good English. He was subsequently turned over to the military police in the Philippines.

During the northern New Guinea campaigns, the lookout for Japanese submarine attempts to resupply scattered forces required around the clock vigilance as indicated here in a PFRA profile note sent along by Captain John Hutson USCG (Ret).

I was CO of the *Belfast* (PF-35) during operations in the SW Pacific. The ship was assigned to an ASW Hunter-Killer task unit with three other ships, 1 frigate and 2 PCs. We were on patrol north of New Guinea attempting to interdict Japanese submarines making supply runs to pockets of resistance along the coast. It was SOP to go to GQ 1h hour before sunrise and 1h hour before sunset. One night we had secured from GQ when our operators found a sonar and radar contact a few miles from our ship. This indicated to me that we had a surfaced submarine or a ship nearby. I sounded the alarm for all hands to go to battle stations and we proceeded to investigate. We tried sending visually the IFF code of the day with no response... As we approached this contact we made out a dark shadow. Our evaluation was that it was a possible derelict. We approached within a few hundred yards and flashed our searchlight at the unknown object and discovered that it was a floating island with trees and shrubbery growing on it. We all breathed a sigh of relief as we secured from GQ. I reported our find to our unit commander as we resumed ASW patrol.

The cleanup operations at Biak and Noemfoor brought on a lot of toing and froing and minor adventures in search of lingering Japanese forces, no better told than through the eyes of a quartermaster. (It was a well-known fact that the two ratings worth consulting for any matter of ship's business were the quartermasters and the leading yeoman). Here, former QM1/c Bob Johnson of the *Eugene* offers a cool-headed view taken from his published story, *Six Months with the Seventh Fleet*, found in The American Neptune, summer 1997.

. . . Reports that Japanese artillery was sighted on nearby Soepiori Island brought a change of duty almost a week later. The whaleboat ferried seven officers from the beach. The frigate proceeded to Rani Island, where they conferred with the native scouts, thence to Sawendi, Soepiori, to bombard the supposed battery. As the ship felt her way between reefs clearly visible in the calm sea, we studied the village through binoculars. Perched on stilts over the water, it looked peaceful and deserted. Nonetheless, the *Eugene* opened fire with 3-inch and 40-mm guns. Some sighted the muzzle flashes of return fire, others thought them to be the frigate's projectiles ricocheting off rocks, certainly there were no shell splashes around the ship. Cease fire was ordered after ten minutes, and then, embarrassingly, the *Eugene* was found to be aground. Her engines were stopped because the screws had struck a coral reef. This mishap was attributed to faulty charts and an ebb tide. Fortunately, the ship had been making little more than steerage way when she grounded.

Refloating her proved to be a simple matter. All hands except those at essential control stations mustered on the forward deck. This living ballast raised the fantail somewhat. "All ahead one-third," "Stop," and the *Eugene* slid off the reef none the worse for the experience. As she headed seaward, the aft 3-inch gun continued the bombardment until Sawendi was out of range....

. .. After enjoying a week at anchor at Mios Woendi, the *Eugene* received orders to support a combat landing. Embarking Army personnel, including the major general commanding the 41st Division and two brigadier generals at Sorido on 6 September, joined by the *Orange* (PF-43) and troop-laden landing craft, she headed for Korrido on Soepiori Island. The force separated the next morning, the *Orange* bombarding Napido preparatory to a landing there, while the *Eugene* closed Korrido and opened fire somewhat later. After shelling the village for twenty minutes, she ceased fire. Aircraft spent a half-hour bombing and strafing before the landing craft put the troops ashore. Apparently there was no opposition--our Army passengers and ship's officers went ashore "to look around" within an hour. All hands had an opportunity to survey the "battlefield" before the *Eugene* returned to Biak.

The Korrido invasion was obviously unimportant, achieving no mention in either Army or Navy operational histories, but one wonders why a single frigate was assigned to provide fire support for such an operation if opposition was expected. Perhaps the Seventh Fleet simply discounted

Army estimates as a matter of course. At any rate, the ship's photographer went out in the whaleboat to record the invasion for posterity, and Captain MacLean had an account prepared for the *Coast Guard Magazine,* in which it appeared before the ship returned to the States...

Eugene spent two days surveying Bepondi Island north of Soepiori in an exercise as quartermaster Johnson put it, "that resulted in a chart on which prominent geographical features were identified by *"Eugene"* names. In due course, this chart was reproduced and distributed to ships of the Seventh Fleet--without the names we had bestowed! We obviously had no right to name bays and headlands of a Dutch possession without permission."

After refueling at Mios Woendi, *Eugene* steamed in company with *Van Buren* to Humboldt Bay for moorings alongside destroyer tender *Dobbin* (AD-3), *Van Buren* tying up outboard of her sister. Three days later Liberty ship SS *Mariscal Sucre,* suffering a steering loss, appeared to be on a course sure to remove the stem of both frigates. Johnson witnessed the developing disaster while mounting the bridge ladder. In the nick of time the Liberty reversed her engine and averted serious damage, although her bow dug into *Van Buren's* port quarter well aft. In a recent letter, former chief pharmacists mate Russell Hitchens relates the same story from the perspective of being aboard the *Van Buren.*

Our ship was rammed at high noon in Hollandia Harbor by a Liberty ship. I was on deck and looking at the ship off in the distance. I noticed the ship getting closer and heading for us. I saw it drop both anchors and go into full astern. That's when I knew we were in trouble. Most of the crew was at noon chow, so I went down to the mess deck and told them to get out of there. They thought I was kidding. Sure enough, the ship hit us in the fantail and cut a great pie wedge in us. We were alongside another frigate moored to a repair ship and did not have steam up. The XO asked me why I didn't blow the collision alarm. I said how could we without steam. The damage was repaired without leaving the harbor.

In the Southwest Pacific the question kept coming up, "How valuable and successful are the 3-inch 50s against aircraft?" Two positive answers come from *Hutchinson* and *San Pedro.* In the "Hutch" newsletter, Fore and Aft, Robert Shaber BM1/c writes:

We were some place in the Islands when we were ordered to escort two navy ships to sea for gun practice. The ships we were escorting were twice our size and had more armament than our ship. They were good, scoring some possibles and a few direct hits on the target towed by the plane. Our commanding officer sent over a request to the senior ship asking if we, too, could have a firing run on the target. Our request was granted and the senior ship sent the following message to the plane: "MAKE A RUN ON THE LITTLE FELLOW." We might have been little but after we fired we made them seem quite small. The plane made a run with the black target trailing behind. We were given the order to OPEN FIRE. All three 3"/50s opened fire with one shot apiece, each hitting the target on the nose. The target fell into the sea.... I had often wondered how the gun crew would perform under fire.... It was a semi-cloudy day when our wish was granted. It came with a bang. Jap planes were overhead and were going to attempt to destroy our convoy .... The silence was broken as the order was given to OPEN FIRE. The first loader slammed each shell home into the breach as fast as the gun could fire...

The word was passed to cease fire--there were no more planes in sight. We had done a job and done it well. The ship was later credited with two sures and two assists...

In answer to a statement in LST SCUTILEBUTT - July/August 1997, by a former LST sailor that the 3-inch 50 was useless against aircraft, Charles Isaacs of *San Pedro* replied:

... As a pointer on a 3-inch 50 in many actions against aircraft I helped earn an enviable record for our ship. The very first night of Pacific Gunnery School firing at a sleeve target our crews and my gun specifically earned the praise via the PA of the Navy officers in the tower. In practice at Cairns, Australia, we again, the *San Pedro* three inchers, knocked off the targets. At Sansapor, at night, with the Army searchlights lighting up an enemy bomber, we got the credit for shooting it down. Later we were informed by the Army that two more planes had crashed and probably from our fire.... In December 1944 while protecting a sinking Liberty, we fought off a heavy attack and though a sister frigate claimed a kill, we insisted the plane didn't smoke until my three incher fired five shells into her. I was on my telescopic sight. However, a senior officer was aboard the other frigate. After the war I received the handwritten log of the captain of that frigate and he graciously had mentioned the *San Pedro* had probably hit it. My point, which I have belabored, is that if well-trained gunners were on the guns, then the guns were great. That goes for the 40mms and 20s as well....

36

David Hendrickson

Morotai, the most northerly of the Halmaheras and about 300 miles northwest of the Vogelkop Peninsula, and Peleliu in the Palaus, about 500 miles due north of the Vogelkop, were invaded on the same day, 15 September 1944. Morotai was a nearly bloodless campaign whereas Peleliu ended as one of the bloodiest. In both cases the islands were softened up by surface ship bombardment and carrier force attack, but on Morotai there was only a small garrison that fled into the mountains. At Peleliu, 14,000 hardened Japanese defenders entrenched in limestone caves awaited the 1st Marine Division. Morotai was the last stepping stone on the way to Leyte, a mere 500 miles to the northwest.

Admiral Barlbey's VII Amphibious Force quickly put ashore 16,000 Army troops on Morotai. Landings began at 0830 without opposition, and the airfield promptly taken. Throughout the day and night light enemy air attacks did no damage. Reinforcement and re-supply landings followed, and by the end of the month 45,000 troops occupied Morotai and Army planes were flying in and out of the CB rebuilt airfield. Participating in the landings, re-supply escort and ASW patrol, were the newly arrived frigates *Carson City* and *Burlington*, assisting *Coronado, El Paso, San Pedro, Long Beach, Glendale* and *Gallup.* Later in October, after delivering British Transports HMS *Arquebus* and HMS *Battleaxe* to the New Hebrides and the Solomons to disembark troops, *Machias* steamed for Morotai to join her escort division sisters, *Allentown, Charlottesville* and *Sandusky.* Then CO of *Sandusky*, Vice Adm. Thomas R. Sargent III (Ret), in a memo remembers *Sandusky's* arrival in the Southwest Pacific:

> ....we transmitted Panama Canal and headed for Bora Bora, Society Islands. After fueling and a little R&R, we sailed for New Guinea. On the way we sighted a mine, avoided by some quick maneuvering and finally arrived in Hollandia, New Guinea. After a few repairs and some fuel we sailed for Morotai and had our first brush with the real war. During an air raid we shot down one Zero, and since we were moored alongside a tanker carrying gasoline, removed the ship to an anchorage at a safe distance. After patrolling the Halamaheras for some time, we sailed to search for a reported submarine but then detached for independent duty to Babelthaup in the Palaus where we picked up a seaplane tender for convoy to Leyte Gulf. ..

Morotai was chosen as a perfect location for a torpedo boat base. Capt. S.S. Bowling, commanding Seventh Fleet PTs, arrived 16 September in tender *Oyster Bay,* together with tender *Mobjack* and boats of Squadrons 9, 10, 18 and 33. Seabees built them an advance base on a small islet offshore from the landing beaches. Up to the end of the war, PTs made nightly patrols that protected Morotai from raids by the Japanese on Halmahera and Eastern Celebes. To complete the base a massive amount of equipment needed to be brought up from New Guinea. *Long Beach,* acting as task group commander, and *San Pedro* were assigned to escort the supply convoy of tugs and tows to Morotai. The following is from the action report submitted by Commander Escort Division 25, USS *Long Beach* to Cominch, 26 September 1944:

A PT base and other floating equipment necessary to operations in forward areas was set up for arrival at Morotai on D+5. This equipment, plus escorts, was designated Task Group 77.7 Reinforcement Group 4-Echelon M-7. The officer in tactical command was Commander A.L. Ford, U.S. Coast Guard and the escorts were the USS LONG BEACH (F) and the USS SAN PEDRO... The assembly point for the reinforcement group was Woendi, a distance of 550 miles from the objective point... The LONG BEACH, with CTG 71.7 on board, arrived at Woendi Harbor at 0800 on 13 September 1944 for the purpose of organizing and conferring with commanding officers of the elements of Echelon M-7... After the conference was adjourned, written orders, instructions and diagrams of dispositions were published and delivered... 14 September 1944. At about 1330 the LONG BEACH and SAN PEDRO commenced screening out of perimeter of rendezvous area south of entrance to Woendi Harbor. Tugs with their tows, proceeded to rendezvous point and forming up. At about 1730 formation was completed and all units were on station. Speed was increased to 4 knots. At about 1830, in spite of the fact that all units were in their proper station prior to darkness, the disposition began to get very ragged, particularly the Army tugs....Following message, the Navy tugs lined themselves up very well. The situation with respect to the Army tugs did not materially improve. 15 September 1944. At 0330 a surface target was picked up dead ahead, range about 9 miles. The LONG BEACH commenced challenging but the challenge was not answered until target was 5 miles distant. .. Upon proper identification target was directed to change course sharply to starboard and this he failed to do. When target was two miles distant units of Echelon M-7 were directed to turn on running lights and target did likewise. The target, which was a merchant ship, passed directly through the convoy but fortunately with no mishap. Because of the composition of Echelon M-7 it is an almost physical impossibility to maneuver this echelon at night to avoid an approaching vessel. At about 1000 the commanding officer of the LONG BEACH, on orders for CTG 77.7 departed the ship to visit each tug with supplementary instructions, emphasizing the necessity for proper keeping of station. If the Army tugs do not keep a better station tonight it is my intention to assign an officer to one of them to take charge for it is feared a serious fouling of tow lines will result unless an improvement is shown.... TG 77.7-Reinforcement Group 4-Echlon M-7 arrived at Morotai on schedule... The equipment was delivered intact. No encounter with the enemy occurred throughout the voyage.

At anchor in Hollandia or Seeadler Harbor or Milne Bay, life could be a dreadful bore and not much better moored to a repair ship other than the opportunity for ice cream. Sweltering conditions below decks encouraged the rigging of hammocks topside and when ashore, sailors were often in search of canvas cots. Aboard *Muskogee,* Frenchie Theriot thought he had it made when he slipped aboard as the proud owner of a purchased cot from a nearby Army unit. He soon had it secured on the fantail under the 20mm clover leaf. After a sweltering fire room watch, Frenchie looked forward to a refreshing shower and a good night's sleep. As he neared his selected spot in the dark, he could just make out a bulging hulk curled up on his recent acquisition. A sharp kick awoke the snoring hulk, who turned out to be Frenchie's water tender mate Tom Johnson. Johnson, a back-country Georgia boy, surrendered his sleep only after a violent argument and advice to Frenchie what he could do with his precious cot. The next night Frenchie found his cot in no condition for restful sleep. The canvas had been sliced into strips, left draped from the wooden frame. He suspected Johnson, but made no accusations for fear that it might have interfered with his coming review for advance in rating. In his unpublished manuscript, (Rub-a-dub-dub) TO SEA IN A TUB, Charlie Isaacs of *San Pedro* tells of marching aboard repair ship *Dobbin* for a shower.

> During repairs our showers were secured and I decided to go aboard the repair ship and enjoy the luxury of fresh, hot water. Carrying soap and towel I started up the connecting gangway. A petty officer with a gun on his hip stopped me.
>
> "Where ya goin' bud?" he asked. (That's what I got for not having on my long pants--or any.)
>
> "I'm going to take a shower," I said.
>
> "Got permission?"
>
> "Permission?"
>
> "Yeah," he sneered, "You don't think you can come aboard any time you like and take a shower, do you?"
>
> "Why not?" I asked innocently, but knowing full well how ships zealously guard their water supply.
>
> "This ain't a bathhouse!" he roared. I misunderstood him at first and was going to argue the point, but then I explained about the men

working on our showers and that I was very dirty. It made little impression.

He said, "If you got troubles –take 'em to the chaplain."

"Look Mac," I said, being tough--it was a wide gangway and I figured I could out run him, "I've got to have a shower. My wife is buying war bonds and paying taxes. That ought to get me something."

This softened him. Maybe he had a wife somewhere, or a war bond, or taxes. Anyway, he leaned close and said, 'Tell you what I'm gonna do. I'll let you go up and see the OD." I was mad enough to take a swing at him, but sane enough not to. I went up topside and approached the officer of the deck.

"Sir," I said, "I am from the USS *San Pedro* and since we are undergoing repairs I'd like permission to take a shower aboard here." He looked me up and down, scratched his head and stared vacantly across the bay. . Perhaps he was dreaming about when he too was young and needed a bath, or perhaps he was running over Navy regulations. But I interrupted whatever he was thinking to ask again.

"I heard you!" he snapped. Then after two minutes he asked, "Do you have to have a shower tonight?"

"I'd like to, sir." I faltered--because now I was somewhat shaken. Perhaps a shower was unnecessary--maybe I was only a slave to tradition.

"Why no! Come back in a couple hours?" he suggested. I knew then that the problem was insurmountable for him and he was trying to get me to return when he went off duty. I steeled myself.

"I need a shower now, sir," I said firmly. "I go on watch soon" I thought I had him cornered, but he played his ace.

"I tell you what I'm going to do," he began. "I'll let you go up and see the executive officer." I started wearily up to the next deck. Suddenly something snapped. Defeat stared me in the face. The executive would only send to the captain, the captain would send me to Admiral Kincaid and then I'd spend days waiting for Kincaid to contact Nimitz and MacArthur to see if I could take a shower bath. I returned to my ship --a forlorn figure, rundown at the soap and a little baggy around the towel--I took a cup of water from the scuttlebutt, brushed my teeth and hit the sack. Miner came by a moment later, dripping wet from a shower. The work had been completed and the showers had been on all during the time I was running around the repair ship.

Hollywood and Navy Special Services provided the one dependable form of recreation. Apart from the occasional two cans of warm beer ashore, the nightly movie when at anchor in a major naval port like Hollandia, viewed on a screen rigged topside, was always a welcome respite. Films were swapped between ships and the rule was that all first run films must be returned before weighing anchor. One story had it that with binoculars handy it was possible to view several movies at the same time depending on distance and angle of sight with other ships. A persistent report had it that the film *Casablanca* had somehow become the private property of frigate *Eugene* and that it had been shown so many times that the entire crew knew the dialogue by heart to the extent that shipmates greeted each other with "Here's looking at you, kid," particularly at two-can beer parties on the beach.

The rapid success of the New Guinea campaigns, the ease of taking Morotai and the stunning destruction of Japanese facilities in the Philippines by Task Force 38 by mid-September 1944, determined MacArthur's and Nimitz's plan to move up operations against Leyte from 20 December to 20 October. On 15 September the Joint Chiefs of Staff granted the request for change of dates. Various elements of Task Force 38 had eradicated Japanese shipping carrying cargo to the Philippines, as carrier attacks were made on the islands of Leyte, Cebu, Panay, Samar, Negros and Bohol, strikes that destroyed nearly 400 aircraft, ten cargo ships, two oilers and many smaller craft. After a 21 September aerial attack on Luzon, very little was left afloat in Manila Bay.

For the Leyte campaign, Vice Admiral Kinkaid was in charge of naval operations. Kinkaid's reorganized Seventh Fleet consisted of three task forces: 77, 78 and 79, with Kinkaid also commanding TF 77, Admiral Barbey TF 78 and Admiral Wilkinson TF 79. Over 700 ships made up the Leyte campaign, of which ten frigates steamed with TF 78 Northern Attack Force, 17-29 October 1944: *Gallup, Bisbee,* TG 78.4 Dinagat Attack Group; *Carson City, Burlington,* TG 78.6 Reinforcement Group One; *Muskogee, San Pedro,* Reinforcement Group Two; *Eugene, El Paso, Van Buren, Orange,* Reinforcement Group Three. Following the October invasion, the primary role for all twenty-one frigates was escort duty back and forth from Hollandia 1500 miles northwest to San Pedro Bay and Tacloban at the northern edge of Leyte Gulf, most trips under sporadic attack by enemy aircraft and occasional kamikaze dives directed at transports, LSTs and large freighters. The fight for Leyte was reasonably complete by March 1945,

The invasion fleet that would land 195,000 Army troops on the shores of Leyte assembled at Seeadler Harbor in the Admiralties and Hollandia on Humboldt Bay. Since the LSTs were capable of only nine-knot speed, initial movement had to start as early as 4 October, less than three weeks after the step up of the landing date had been made and only 16 days before A-day.

19a

Task Organization for the Invasion of Leyte
17-25 October 1944

TF 78 NORTHERN ATTACK FORCE
Rear Admiral Daniel E. Barbey

TG 78.4 DINAGAT ATTACK GROUP, Rear Admiral Struble in HUGHES, embarking 6th Ranger Battalion, Lt. Col. H.A. Mucci and Co. B 21st Infantry.

Destroyer transports KILTY Lt. L.G Benson USNR, SCHLEY Lt. Cdr. E.T. Farley USNR, WARD Lt. R.E. Farwell USNR, HERBERT Lt. G.S. Hewitt USNR, CROSBY Lt. G.G. Moffatt USNR, fleet tug CHICKISAW Lt. L.C. Olsen NSNR.

Escorts: destroyers LANG Cdr. H Payson, STACK Cdr. R.E. Wheeler; frigates* GALLUP Lt. Cdr. C.M. Opp, BISBEE Cdr. J.P. German.

Bombardment Group, Rear Admiral R.W. Hayler, Light cruisers DENVER, COLUMBIA AND DesDiv 112.
- - - - - - - - - - - - - -

TG 78.6 REINFORCEMENT GROUP ONE, Captain S.P. Jenkins (Arrived 22 October)

Attack transports CRESCENT CITY Capt. L.L. Rowe, WARREN Capt. W.A. McHale USNR, WINDSOR Capt. D.C. Woodward USNR, CALLAWAY Capt. D.C. McNeil USCG, LEON Capt. B.B Adell, SUMTER Cdr. J.T. O'Pry USNR; transport STORM KING Cdr. H.J. Hansen; cargo ship JUPITER Cdr. J.M. Bristol; repair ship ACHILLES Lt. C.O. Smith USNR; 4 merchant ships.

32 LST from Flotilla 8, Capt. O.R. Swigart; 12 LCI.

Escort, Captain E.A. Solomons (Comdesron 2) Destroyers MORRIS Lt. Cdr. R.V. Wheeler, HOWORTH Cdr. E.S. Burns, STEVENS, Cdr. W.M. Rakow, MUSTIN Lt. Cdr. J.G. Hughes; Frigates CARSON CITY Cdr. H.B. Roberts USCG, BURLINGTON Cdr. E.V. Carlson USCG.
- - - - - - - - - - - - - -

TG 78.7 REINFORCEMENT GROUP TWO, Captain J.K.B. Ginder (Arrived 24 October)

33 LST of Flotilla 14, Capt. E.A. Seay, 24 Liberty and other merchant marine freighters; 12 units of Service Force Seventh Fleet.

Escort, Captain Ginder (Comdesron 21) Destroyers NICHOLAS Cdr. T.S. Keith, O'BANNON Cdr. R.W. Smith, HOPEWELL Cdr. W.S. Rodimon, TAYLOR Cdr. N.J. Frank; Frigates MUSKOGEE Cdr. R.E. Mroczkowski USCG, SAN PEDRO Lt. H.L. Sutherland USCGR.
- - - - - - - - - - - - - -

TG 78.8 REINFORCEMENT GROUP THREE, Cdr. J.L. Steinmetz USCG (Arrived 29 October)

6 LST, 19 Liberty and Victory ships; units of Service Force Seventh Fleet.

Escort, Captain W.M. Cole (Comdesron 5) Destroyers FLUSSER Cdr. T.R. Vogeley, MAHAN Cdr. E.G. Cambell, DRAYTON Cdr. R.S. Craighill, SMITH Cdr. F.V. List, LAMSON Cdr. J.V. Noel; Frigates EUGENE Cdr. C.R. MacLean USCG, EL PASO Cdr. R.J. Barromey USCG, VAN BUREN Cdr. C.B. Arrington USCG, ORANGE Cdr. J.A. Dirks USCG.
- - - - - - - - - - - - - -

* These frigates became Harbor Control Group in San Pedro Bay under Capt. F.W. Benson.

(MacArthur chose the use of A-day since D-day was fixed in the public's mind with Normandy.) At the time, much of Admiral Barbey's fleet was winding up work at Morotai, but as he put it, "By careful arrangement of the shipping schedule, enough time was obtained between operations to fuel and take on stores, but little else. This has been the customary experience of the VII Amphibious Force which has carried out fourteen assault landings and their resupply in the previous twelve months." The northward movement was underway on 10 October when the Minesweeping and Hydrographic Group departed Manus, followed on 12 October by the Dinagat Attack Group from Hollandia, all aiming for a position called "Point Fin" off the entrance to Leyte Gulf, 1250 miles from Hollandia, through which all of the Expeditionary Force must pass.

Quartermaster Bob Johnson speculates here why the *Eugene* was denied participation in the Dinagat Attack Group.

> . . . Commodore Steinmetz returned from a conference, bringing a chart showing projected landing beaches, which he directed me to post in the chartroom. It was stamped "Confidential," but an order from the commodore was not mine to question. A few days later, Rear Admiral Daniel E. Barbey, commanding the Seventh Fleet amphibious forces, visited the ship. Looking into the chartroom, he noticed the chart. 'Who put that there?" "The commodore, sir." "Get the commodore." After informing the division commander that the admiral wished to see him, I paused in the wheelhouse. When I returned to the chartroom, both officers had gone -- and so had the chart.
>
> I have since wondered if Admiral Barbey's purpose had been to determine the *Eugene's* readiness for a special mission, that of screening the fast transports that landed Rangers on the islands off Leyte before the invasion. If so, Commodore Steinmetz's indiscretion may have been a factor in the choice of the *Bisbee* (PF-46) and the *Gallup* (PF-47) for the mission...

As it was on 17-18 October 1944, frigates *Bisbee* and *Gallup* participated in the landing of the US Rangers on the islands of Dinagat and Homohon, which guarded the entrance to Leyte Gulf. The following, edited for length, is an account submitted by William Tyrrel and Clyde Stackhouse of USS *Gallup* (PF-47):

> Near the middle of October, the scuttlebutt was flying fast and furious aboard the *Gallup*, on duty with the 7th Fleet since 31 May 1944. Something was definitely in the wind something big. But common sense kept rearing its ugly head and giving rise to thoughts; "A frigate is no battleship,"

not by a long sight. Granted, something big is going to take place but you won't get in on it till weeks after the enemy has been pretty well cleaned out. Even if they do include frigates, your chances will be slim. Disturbing thoughts, but things began to happen that caused the scuttlebutt to fly all the more fast and furious. Late in the afternoon of 8 October, we were suddenly ordered to get underway in company with a division of destroyers --pretty fast company for a lowly frigate. We spent the afternoon and night whipping off maneuvers at high speed, returning to port the next morning at sunup.

The morning of 12 October slipped by. At 1630 "All hands secure for sea and prepare to get underway" sounded over the PA. The whaleboat was taken aboard, ladder rigged in, anchor aweigh and we were headed seaward. Now there was no scuttlebutt; all hands waited quietly expectant. We knew that once clear of port the captain would announce our destination. We did not have to wait long. "Attention all hands. Our destination is the Philippines." the intake of breath down a couple hundred throats was clearly audible from the bridge. Then there were cheers. It was the dream of every man in the Pacific. We were going to land on Philippine soil, not on D-day, but THREE DAYS BEFORE D-DAY. "Our group will land on 17 October on Dinagat Island and Homohon Island," the captain continued, "And we'll be followed on 20 October by the major landings on Leyte Island. Directly upon our efforts will depend the success of the entire operation, the lives of thousands of men, the safety of hundreds of ships. The two islands on which we will establish beachheads command the approaches to Leyte. We will land Army Rangers to knock out shore batteries, radio stations, and radar installations. Leyte Gulf is heavily mined. Our job is to clear out every mine. I expect every man to perform his duty to perfection." Was it mere coincidence or just plain good luck that this ship of all the frigates and destroyers available was included in the battle plan? Some weeks before, the fire support provided by the *Gallup* covering landings in New Guinea resulted in the awarding of a letter of commendation which, as it made the rounds, collected the endorsement of assorted generals and admirals, including General MacArthur. The letter stressed "The enthusiasm and zeal displayed by the men and officers of the USS *Gallup* and the extremely heavy and accurate gunfire with which this ship supported the landings."

October 12 and 13 passed uneventfully, weather clear, smooth sailing until the afternoon of 14 October brought overcast skies, rain squalls and a heavy swell that pointed to the approaching typhoon. As night came on, the typhoon struck. Torrential rain, driven by ever increasing wind lashed the ship and destroyed visibility. Seas broke as high as the flying bridge, forty feet above the surface. Occasional enemy snooper planes were picked up by radar, but the weather protected us from their prying. Typhoons invariably pass over in ten hours; however, our task force and the typhoon traveled the same course at about the same speed. As a result we were kicked and blown about night and day.

Somewhere off Palau we rendezvoused with a fleet of tankers, refueled, and were joined by several minesweeper flotillas. We were temporarily detached to carry secret dispatches to the huge force of battleships, cruisers, escort carriers and destroyers that were to support the Leyte landings. Rejoining our task force and with the typhoon still raging, we set course to the northwest, bucking wind and sea that swamped some of the smaller units and increased the danger of collision in the dark.

At 0430, 17 October, our forces split; our group to remain off Dinagat Island, the other to make for Homonhon Island, H-hour as soon as possible after the break of day. The general alarm brought all hands to battle stations, guns manned and ready, hearts pounding, stomachs tied in knots and then the storm blew by, wind and rain died away and visibility increased to five miles. We took our attack formation, first a destroyer, then the *Gallup* followed by another destroyer and then the Ranger carrying attack transports. A couple thousand yards ahead were the minesweepers with paravanes streamed. We followed a course roughly parallel to the north coast of Dinagat. Our first target area, Desolation Point arose in the distance. A final check of photos and charts and then the oft-rehearsed orders to the gun crews--set all ammunition on superquick--all guns shift to remote control, master key fire--load and stand by--train on target--range eight three double oh--range seven seven double oh--slowly the range decreased. All eyes were on the destroyer up ahead. Her first salvo was to be the signal to open fire. Suddenly her guns blazed a ranging salvo. Aboard the *Gallup* the salvo buzzer sounded--a firing key was closed--our first salvo roared out--and landed on target! Again fate had a hand in our destiny for the tin-can's first salvo fell short, making us the first ship to land a blow in the liberation of the Philippines and the first Coast Guard-manned ship to fire a liberation salvo. (editor's note -Morison in Leyte p.116 gives first salvo honors to cruiser *Denver* firing on Suluan Island at 0800 17 October.) An hour later Dinagat Island became the first of the Philippines to be liberated. The *"Gal* then had

45

other work to do. We received orders to fall in astern of the minesweeps and act as "mine destruction vessel." A mine was reported to port, a rusty iron globe studded with detonator spikes, loaded with enough high explosives to blow the bow off a ship. Because of rough water, we closed in to 150 yards. The 20mms found the range and the resulting blast splattered shrapnel off our helmets. A second mine to port took two runs to destroy because the typhoon was back and visibility greatly reduced. But now our minesweeps were nowhere in sight. At all ahead full in what we thought was the 300 yard wide swept channel, we soon picked up a radar contact on ships we believed our lost minesweeps. We closed the distance and by voice radio found that we had been chasing a group that had been assigned to clear another area. We had been barging through an unswept minefield for about two hours at full speed. We came about and got the hell out of there --but fast.

Early on the morning of the 19th, we began to collect hydrographical data, plotting the set and drift of a racing tidal current, computing the time of flood and ebb slack tides. During the day we also assisted in establishing lights to guide the invasion force. During the night we patrolled close to Dinagat and watched silhouettes of the Leyte attack group ghost along through the dark to attack at dawn. We felt a bit smug as we watched the huge force stream by. After all we had been here in the Philippines for three days. We also felt somewhat comforted. It was a good feeling to realize that the big boys were now playing in our backyard.

With the bombardment going on a few miles away, and voice radio and the sound and sight of gunfire bringing us a blow by blow description of the Leyte attack, we took up duties similar to a traffic cop in the center of the swept channel within Leyte Gulf. The next days brought little change in the routine to which we'd already become accustomed. However, radio reports on the 23rd and 24th indicated that a large Jap naval force was headed in our direction. (Editor's note -the Battle for Leyte Gulf, 24-29 October --Battle of Surigao Strait, Battle off Samar, Battle off Cape Engano). At about 0230, 24 October, the first sighting report screamed out over the radio, "Enemy force of two battleships, six or seven cruisers, and undetermined number of destroyers sighted five miles off Tunga Point." From our ringside seat only a few miles away, we hear the Seventh Fleet maneuvering to intercept. Orders cracked over the radio. Half an hour later the battle began, the first time in the war that a large number of ships of opposing naval forces had met to slug it out. From our uncomfortably close vantage point we could see ships silhouetted against the backdrop of gunfire and torpedo blasts. We had little trouble visualizing the entire battle. Danger seemed to have passed by noon on the 26th, but a large Jap force was soon reported almost at the entrance of San Bernardino Straits. The fleet passed through the straits and attacked a number of our escort carriers steaming but a few miles from our position at the entrance to Leyte Gulf. Another page of history was filled on the afternoon of 26 October of a superior naval force put to rout by the gallant men of our light carriers and their escorts.

Since the 26th of October, bombing and strafing raids and occasional attempts to sink our ships by suicide dives have been the daily routine. The *Gallup,* among the first combat vessels in the return to the Philippines, earned a distinction we would gladly trade for a month's accumulation of mail that awaits us a thousand miles or so away, back at our mail base. Except for fleeting moments when the thrill of battle puts to rout all other feelings and emotions, WAR IS INDEED AN UTTER BORE!

With the loss of three battleships, four carriers, ten cruisers and eleven destroyers in the Battle for Leyte Gulf, the Japanese Navy, as a fighting fleet, ceased to exist. The enemy turned to increasing aerial attack and desperation kamikaze assaults upon resupply and reinforcement convoys steaming from Hollandia to Leyte. Following the successful landings on the morning of the 20th of October, MacArthur waded ashore near Tacloban on the afternoon to pronounce, "People of the Philippines, I have returned. By the grace of God our forces stand again on Philippine soil. .." Now began the bitter slog through Leyte and points north to Luzon, success dependent on an unbroken supply line from Hollandia. As planned for A-day, transports carried just enough cargo to be unloaded by daylight the first day, so that they could retire that night and avoid air attack. Shipping was barely adequate owing to the demands of the European Theater. MacArthur and the Seventh Fleet could afford no losses. 12,000 tons of supplies were landed on Beach Red and Beach White on 20 October, and all of Admiral Barbey's transports and cargo ships were ready to depart for Hollandia at 1800. Not a bad day's work.

During the days of beachhead expansion, 21-23 October, skies were never more than half overcast, winds light, enemy air raids on Leyte Gulf few and planes registered on radar mostly observing. One nasty blow occurred at dawn on the 21st, when a Japanese plane crashed into the foremast of HMAS *Australia,* killing the captain and 19 ratings. Under escort, *Australia* retired to Manus for repairs. Admiral Barbey's initial assault shipping cleared the Gulf by dark on the 20th making way on the beaches for Reinforcement Group One which arrived on the 22nd, composed of six attack transports, five cargo ships, thirty-one LSTs and a repair ship, escorted by four destroyers and frigates *Carson City* and *Burlington,* the first frigates to Leyte Gulf to follow *Bisbee* and *Gallup* of the Dinagat Attack

Group. With unloading operations working smoothly, most of Group One unloaded quickly and were able to depart for the return to Hollandia by 1700 the same day. All in good time, for Reinforcement Group Two arrived on the morning of October 24, comprised of thirty-three LSTs, twenty-four cargo ships and twelve units of Service Force Seventh Fleet, escorted by four destroyers and frigates *Muskogee* and *San Pedro.* Unloading began shortly after daybreak, but only a few ships managed to unload and depart on the 24th; most had to sit tight for the great sea battles of Leyte Gulf, 24-25 October. Enemy air attacks began in mid-morning on the 24th, aiming at Seventh Fleet battleships, cruisers and destroyers in Leyte Gulf preparing to deploy for night battle with the enemy fleet advancing through Surigao Strait. With the entire Gulf under "Flash Red," *San Pedro* and *Muskogee* joined the destroyers in a circling dash around the fleet, laying a smoke screen of black smoke pouring from the stack and white smoke curling from the fantail mounted chemical tanks. Sea battles notwithstanding, Seventh Fleet amphibious division of TF 78 Northern Attack Force successfully landed 80,900 men and 114,900 tons of supplies and equipment by the end of the day 25 October. When the fleet deployed to meet the enemy in the three battles of Leyte Gulf, it appeared that the inner Gulf and San Pedro Bay were abandoned in the face of possible retaliation to defense by five patrol frigates: *San Pedro, Muskogee, Bisbee, Gallup* and *Coronado,* which had mysteriously arrived to join her sisters.

But help was on its way, just in case the Japanese fleet had not all but vanished in the battles. On 23 October, Reinforcement Group Three departed Hollandia for Leyte, six LSTs and nineteen cargo vessels escorted by five destroyers and action-hungry frigates of CortDiv 29, *Eugene, El Paso, Van Buren* and *Orange.* The action that greeted Group Three upon arrival at Leyte on the 29th was not so much the Japanese as it was a full-force typhoon. Full-powered ships put out to sea to ride out the typhoon. The frigates (apparently not considered full powered vessels) rode out the high winds at anchor along with the freighters and transports in San Pedro Bay, all vessels subject to dragging anchors. *Eugene's* situation was particularly dicey with only one anchor, the other jammed in its hawsepipe. In howling wind and sheets of rain *Eugene* weighed her dragging anchor and stood out of San Pedro Bay, only to find a drifting LCVP which she took in tow for return to the boat pool at Dulag when the storm abated.

For the next few days before returning to Hollandia, *Eugene, Orange* and *San Pedro* patrolled in Leyte Gulf. Condition Red was normal condition with sporadic attack by Japanese aircraft aimed at the transports and cargo ships. On 1 November a flight of Japanese torpedo planes penetrated air cover to hit an element of the fleet. On patrol, *Eugene* spotted a black column of smoke that marked the end of destroyer *Abner Read,* hit by a Kamikaze which crashed her deck and started a fire that exploded the destroyer's magazines. Relieved by destroyers on 3 November, *Eugene* sailed that afternoon with a convoy bound for Hollandia.

David Hendrickson

23a

The following is taken from Charles Isaacs' March 1992 *Sea Classics* magazine story, "The Forgotten Fleet of WWII," in which Charlie describes action in Leyte Gulf on D-day plus four, 24 October 1944.

- - - - - - - - - - - - - - - - - - - -

As one of the escorts to a gigantic convoy of men and material, our frigate, the USS San Pedro, made its way through the partially swept mine field and arrived at Leyte on D plus four day. Reports said the first landings had come off almost painlessly, the beachheads were secure and the town of San Pablo was liberated. In the harbor, a task force of battleships, cruisers, and destroyers shifted restlessly. Our LSTs, like a caravan of camels, plodded on into the beach with their thousands of reinforcements. The lumbering tankers fell out of line and were immediately set upon by thirsty cruisers. It was all very peaceful.

"Looks like another Hollandia," a gunner said dejectedly. Suddenly, a voice over the speaker system bellowed, "Flash Red!" and all guns went on sharp alert. Destroyers whipped about laying smoke screens. The USS *San Pedro* and the USS *Muskogee* raced in circles around battleships, cruisers, and communication ships. Pitch black smoke poured from our stack — white smoke spewed from the after chemical tanks, curling in with the other like a continuous black and white barber pole. Through an arch of white smoke we saw the *Muskogee* laying a heavy screen ahead of a battleship that dwarfed the frigate. At 0830, the Japanese bombers arrived. They hit first at the transport area, sinking one Liberty ship and laying an orange-yellow explosion on another Liberty, putting 20 feet of water in her engine room. Ack-ack and tracers split the sky and a plane exploded in mid-air. Another, diving down at a tanker, burst into flames and crashed into the bay, sending up for an instant a strange fountain of water and fire. In between the milling battleships, cruisers, cans, and frigates was the incongruous sight of two native canoes, their occupants paddling one way, then the other.

"The Filipino navy is catching hell," a lookout laughed, albeit nervously. The enemy planes, those that were left, plunged away through the clouds and we began a roving patrol of the bay. A life raft was sighted bobbing on the waves and in a few minutes we came alongside. A pilot lay stretched across the raft.

"You Japanese?" someone yelled down from a gun tub.

"Hell, no," the flyer shouted, taking off his cap to disclose cropped blond hair. "I'm a Norwegian from Minnesota!" We brought him aboard and learned he was a spotter pilot who had been shot down

the day before, landing on a point of land still occupied by the enemy. Hearing them coming his way, he slipped out with his raft and had drifted for hours under the blistering sun.

We churned in great circles in the center of the bay and within minutes, the second raid started. LSTs and cans opened up and shrapnel from their guns cut the water around us with a slicing splash. Bombs stabbed holes in the water around the LSTs. As the planes swept over, we opened with an antiaircraft barrage and more bombs lifted frightening geysers of water off our stern.

The bombers came back repeatedly, and repeatedly they were knocked down or driven off. Night came and it was worse. Like mosquitos, you didn't know where they were until they stung. A tanker received a hit on its port bow, the awesome explosion accompanied by flame that billowed horribly into the dark sky. When the raids suddenly ceased, the silence seemed to roar almost as loudly. Then the army on the beach began an artillery barrage as they continued driving the Japanese back to the hills.

The next day was the 25th and it was the same thing. Bombs and barrage. There was almost a raid an hour. In a sun so hot we couldn't touch the tops of our steel helmets, our eyes bloodshot from searching the smoldering sky, our lips cracked, we stayed at the guns. Almost like a blessing, a rain would intermittently shower down, strangely enough, out of the still sunny sky. The rain didn't stop the enemy. This was their inning and they were punching hard and fast. An LST was hit, then a destroyer caught a bomb, killing six men. Things were tough enough without the next news we learned. A huge Japanese task force

was approaching Leyte Island. We noticed the fleet moving out. Soon, the only destroyers left in the bay were too crippled to move. The Coast Guard-manned frigates, USS *San Pedro*, USS *Muskogee*, now joined by the USS *Coronado*, were the only warships left guarding the transports, LSTs, cargo ships, communication and headquarters ships, the nerve centers of the invasion forces. News correspondents in the area were already talking of a "Pacific Dunkirk." It was reported that Japanese troop transports were to follow the battle fleet to San Pedro Bay.

The American task group from the harbor was moving against the Japanese force coming up from the south. It was a race against time for Halsey's fleet to catch the Japanese armada speeding down from the north before it reached the bay and trapped our forces there.

What could three frigates, armed against aircraft and submarines, do against battleships and cruisers, or even destroyers which could lay out of range and pulverize us with their five to 16-inch guns. Yet in these crucial hours, fully aware of the dangerous, powerful enemy now only 40 or 50 miles away, there was no panic, no outward sign of fear, only grim determination.

The raids let up a little that night, giving us more time to worry about the approaching enemy force. Before dawn on the 26th, a man from the radio shack came up and told us a radio news broadcast had said that a small force of D.E.s had been left guarding San Pedro Bay. "Oh, well," a hot shell man shrugged, "I'd just as soon they call us D.E.s. My folks would worry if they knew the Coast Guard Frigates were in Leyte Gulf."

Convoys from Hollandia continued to deliver troops, supplies and equipment to Leyte throughout November and December. A large share of the escort duty fell to the frigates which had their moments of excitement. On 12 November a convoy of thirty-five LSTs, thirty freighters and seven oilers arrived in Leyte Gulf under escort by *Ogden*, *Burlington* and others, the convoy pursued relentlessly by enemy bombers and observation planes. During the re-supply landing a Kamikaze crashed *LST*-66, killing eight men and

49

wounding fourteen. Nearby, *LST-68* and *LST*-168 claimed three planes in the attack. Offshore, *Ogden* and *Burlington* patrolled as anti-aircraft screen for re-supply ships awaiting unloading off Dulag. In a day that must have set a near record for ferocity of attack, two cargo vessels suffered direct bomb hits and at the end of the day *Ogden* proudly accepted the well-earned message:

FROM COMMANDER ESCORT DIVISION TWENTY FIVE, U.S.S. LONG BEACH, FLAGSHIP. THE OGDEN PF-39 IS TO BE COMMENDED FOR SHOOTING DOWN THREE (3) ENEMY PLANES, DULAG, LEYTE ISLAND, PHILIPPINE ISLANDS.

5 December 1944, from the rough log of USS *Coronado* (PF-38) enroute to Leyte Gulf escorting Task Unit 76.4.7 in company with *Glendale* (PF-36), *Belfast* (PF-35), *Ogden* (PF-39) and *San Pedro* (PF-37). Position 1200 06.42.7 N 133.24.0 E. ---CO Comdr. Ned W. Sprow.

At 0600 commenced zig-zagging, plan #15. At 0800 went to general quarters when it was observed that starboard side of convoy was under attack by an enemy bomber. Bombs were dropped but no damage was reported and enemy plane escaped. Secured from general quarters at 0950... At 1216 sighted enemy plane, believed to be OSCAR, heading in on port side of convoy from 2OQoT, very low. Went to general quarters immediately and commenced firing port weapons. As plane passed ahead at 1219, he launched a torpedo which hit the stern of the SS Antoine Saugrain. Cease firing was ordered as plane crossed our bow from port to starboard about 3000 yards ahead. A few rounds were fired from the forward starboard automatic weapons. One (1) of these rounds from #23, 20mm gun, mounted on the starboard wing of the signal bridge hit and instantly killed Lieut. (jg) Godfery H. Constable, USCGR who had placed himself in the line of fire of this gun and was not observed there by the crew when the gun was fired. Lieut. (jg) John D. Burrows, USCGR; Brehm, Ruben (665-029) S1/c, USCGR; Anderson, Francis (535-638) FC3lc, USCGR; Brewer, Robert C. (588-726) S1/c USCGR, were all slightly injured by steel splinters when the 20mm shell burst in hitting Lieut. (jg) Constable. All received medical attention.

At 1226 commenced firing on another OSCAR making torpedo run on convoy from 290°T. The ANTOINE SAUGRAIN by this time dead in the water, was again hit, this time in the No.2 hold. The SAUGRAIN commenced to settle slowly forward and started taking a starboard list. She was very quickly abandoned by all hands. Put boat over and commenced picking up survivors, as did also the L T 454 and the USS SAN PEDRO. All survivors picked up by the LT 454 were transferred to the

CORONADO and the SAN PEDRO in order to permit the L T 454 to take the SAUGRAIN in tow if such action was indicated.

The CORONADO received on board 233 Army troops including Lt. Col. Wm. H Hubbard, USA CAC, Commander of troops, 9 enlisted men of the Navy gun crew and 31 merchant seamen including the master of the SAUGRAIN, A. Van Cromphant, a total of 263 men.... At 1700 the USS SAN PEDRO was directed to return to the main body. She had on board approximately 185 survivors. A check up later failed to reveal any loss of life among the personnel on board the SAUGRAIN

The SAUGRAIN continued to float. It commenced to appear to me that she had reached a state of equilibrium and it appeared that she might be towed to port. My decision was influenced by the fact that she had in her cargo a large amount of radar searchlight and other radar equipment of a vitally needed nature. She was also reported to have on board a vast amount of mail. At any rate she refused to sink. At 1700 the L T 454 was ordered to take her in tow, stern first and at 1820 she was in tow. It was dark by now. LT 454 continued towing throughout the night at the amazing speed of 5.5 knots. USS CORONADO 6 December 1944

Daylight was anxiously awaited to observe the condition of the cripple. Just before daylight the USS QUAPAW joined and was ordered to standby in case her assistance was needed thru Dinagat Strait. SS SAUGRAIN looked just about the same, except she might have been slightly deeper forward. She was a cinch to make it if the Nips left her alone. They didn't. ... At 0800 relieved of escort by USS HALFORD. Proceeded at best speed to San Pedro Bay where arrived and anchored at 1530. All Army and merchant personnel departed the ship before dark. At 1656 the body of Lieut. (jg) Godfrey H. Constable was transported ashore for burial. .. At about 1600 a message was heard from USS HALFORD to the effect that mission was unsuccessful. It was later learned from the commanding officer of LT 454 that SAUGRAIN received a third torpedo and quickly sank....

As the year 1944 drew to a close, the days were numbered for the frigates in the Southwest Pacific. The Pacific War was rapidly moving north ever closer to Japan in waters where fast task forces and big guns ruled the sea and long range bombers raided the Japanese homeland from the Marianas. By December, the 24 knot steam-powered DEs with 5-inch guns made their first appearance in Equatorial waters to replace the 20 knot frigates. CortDiv 43 was first to make the break and head north to cooler seas. *Rockford* made an early escape on 18 October bound for Pearl Harbor and San Francisco for major repairs. *Gallup, Bisbee, Burlington, Muskogee* and *Carson City* steamed into Pearl Harbor on 15 December, and as bad luck would have it, after a short availability, *Muskogee, Carson City* and *Bisbee* made straight for Dutch Harbor and the cold Bering Sea. *Burlington* and *Gallup* had the good luck of Mare Island availability until along with *Rockford* they departed San Francisco, sentenced also to the Bering Sea, joining their sisters in January 1945. CortDiv 43 lingered in the Aleutians until making for Seattle in July and refit for the USSR Lend-Lease scheme.

CortDiv 25, made up of the six frigates that collectively earned the most battle stars and the first on scene in New Guinea were the next to leave. Led off by 5 star *Glendale* on 8 December, followed by *Long Beach, Coronado, San Pedro, Ogden* and *Belfast,* CortDiv 25 made for a Boston arrival on 24 January 1945, and refit for transfer to the USSR at Cold Bay, Alaska, later in the summer.

25a

Transposed by the editor from the handwritten draft submitted by:

Lt. Richard N. Hofmaster, USS *Belfast* (PF-35)

The *Belfast* was part of a large convoy attacked off Mindanao on 5 December 1944. I had just taken my place as senior watch officer at 0800 when word came from CIC that enemy planes were approaching. General quarters was sounded and the ship took May Day station alongside the convoy, closing at flank speed.

Almost as soon as they were sighted, one of the kamikazes peeled off, heading for the transport SS *Antoine Saugrain*, steaming about 75 yards on our port beam. I can still remember seeing the pilot's clenched fist salute or whatever and also that we brought that fist down with some pretty good hits. As the kamikaze was passing over, out of the corner of my eye, I saw someone run towards the stern from about midship, when a torpedo bomber came in from the other side and literally broke the transports back, blowing this fellow into the air and presumably into the water. I can remember feeling sorry for him as we could not stop and aid his ship right then.

Well - after the war, I returned to Ohio State University in January 1946. One day I was sitting by my friend, Emerson Niswander, on the third floor of the Botany-Zoology Bldg. Emerson was from Bluffton about 35 miles from my home near Fostoria, Ohio. Most of us had been in the service and were prone to reminisce a bit. On this day Emerson mentioned getting 'Survivor's Leave,' and I asked him, how come? "Well." he said, "I was on this transport named something like sauerkraut off Mindanoa in the Philippines in early December 1944, when a Jap Kamikaze came in over the escort vessel next to us and I ran toward the stern to get away from him. About the same time a torpedo bomber hit us from the other side." I told him I was there too! This tale is verifiable as we still keep in touch.

- -

The following is from When the Boys Leave Home, the war experiences of Lee Kolankiewicz, 2773rd U.S. Army Engineers, aboard SS *Antoine Saugrain*, bound for the Philippines from Hollandia, New Guinea .

. . . Suddenly there was a terrific blast behind us. For just a fraction of a second I realized I was in midair, as if suspended there. Then I came crashing back on deck. I couldn't understand what had been hit. . . . Someone yelled down from above on the main deck if everyone was alright. Several "Yeas" were shouted back. Moments passed, and then we were ordered to our abandon ship stations. . . . Then I realized we weren't moving. One of the crew passed by and I asked what had happened. He said, "That was a Jap torpedo bomber. The torpedo sheered off our rudder and propeller. We're sitting ducks!"

So then we knew. . . and realized. . . .and began to wait for what we knew would come. The *Antoine Saugrain* was already beginning to settle slowly, completely dead in the water.. . . The rest of the convoy had continued. . . .

Then I sighted one plane, just a dot bearing down on us. . . . I can't explain why I didn't take cover. . . Instead, I stood in the middle of the hatch cover watching the plane coming in at mast height. . . . Several hundred yards from the ship something big and black dropped from the belly of the plane. I yelled,"He dropped it! He dropped it!" . . .Then the blast came, bone jarring. Only seconds passed before the ship's whistle tooted the abandon ship signal. . . I managed to get to the raft, then climb aboard it, but I simply did not have the strength to climb to the deck of the rescue vessel. I was pulled aboard the U.S. Coast Guard frigate *Coronado*. There was another frigate, the *San Pedro*, picking up survivors from the starboard side of the *Saugrain*. At this time we did not know whether all are men had been picked up, or how many casualties. There were about 200 survivors on the *Coronado*.. . .

Abandon ship, SS Antoine Saugrain, Leyte Gulf, 5 December 1944

Last moments of SS Antoine Saugrain, Leyte Gulf, 6 December 1944, from tow vessel LT 454

CortDiv 29 made up of *Eugene, El Paso, Van Buren* and *Orange,* made a clean escape by early January 1945. *Van Buren* reached Pearl Harbor at the end of December, where she remained as a training vessel for Pacific destroyers until June 1945, then to San Francisco for weather duty. *Orange* arrived at Mare Island for availability in February, then to San Diego to serve as a training vessel at the West Coast Sound School until December when she departed for Hawaii weather duty. *Eugene* and *El Paso* cleared Seeadler Harbor on 8 January 1945 for the long passage to Bora Bora and on to transit the Panama Canal on 5 February, and finally to New York on 14 February to be greeted by snow and 10° temperatures. Following availability at Brooklyn Navy Yard the two frigates later stood out of New York with a convoy bound for the Mediterranean. Upon return both ships were converted to weather ships, *Eugene* remaining in the Atlantic to serve on stations out of Boston and Argentia, Newfoundland, while *El Paso* made the long journey back to her old home waters for weather patrol out of Leyte.

The last of the California frigates in New Guinea, *Hutchinson,* rather than steam north for home, headed south on 28 December 1944, slipping by Sydney and Melbourne, through the Bass Straits and on to Fremantle to join up with *Corpus Christi* and Task Force 71 for Indian Ocean service until August 1945. The two frigates departed Fremantle for Pearl Harbor via Manus, arriving 24 September, and the next day both made for San Pedro and availability before reporting for weather duty, *Corpus Christi* out of San Francisco and *Hutchinson* on Station Able out of Seattle.

CortDiv 33, *Sandusky, Machias, Allentown* and *Charlottesville,* remained in New Guinea/Philippine waters until early March 1945, primarily engaged in escort duty of re-supply and reinforcement units from Hollandia to Leyte. Convoys were numerous and large and Leyte was the marshaling site as American forces moved north to Mindoro and Luzon. Between late November and the end of February, *Allentown* and *Sandusky* crossed the Equator more than a dozen times, plodding back and forth from Hollandia to Leyte. The two frigates escorted ships to Mindoro, Subic Bay and as far north on Luzon as Ungayen Gulf in late February 1945. *Sandusky's* last 'ping patrol' assignment occurred off Lingayen Gulf in the last days of February. All four frigates of CortDiv 33 were on their way to Hawaii on 6 March via Ulithi Atoll in the Carolines and Eniwetok Atoll in the Marshalls. *Sandusky* joined a fast convoy from Ulithi to Hawaii while *Allentown* joined up with *Machias* at Eniwetok for a slower trip to Pearl Harbor. The three plus *Charlottesville* stood out of Pearl Harbor on 31 March for a 7 April arrival in Seattle for refit en route to Cold Bay and transfer to the USSR on 12 July 1945. So much for the service of the warm water frigates. Now we move on to those that served in much colder climes.

THE U.S. COAST GUARD IN WORLD WAR II

COAST GUARD-MANNED VESSELS ENGAGED IN AMPHIBIOUS OPERATIONS IN PACIFIC—1944

Name of Vessel	Saidor	Marshalls—Kwajalein	Majuro	Eniwetok	Green Island	Admiralty Islands	St. Mathias Islands	Hollandia	Wakde Island	Biak Island	Marianas—Saipan	Guam	Tinian	Noemfoor Island	Cape Sansapor	Peleliu	Angaur	Morotai	Leyte	Mindoro
Allentown																			X	
Aquarius		X	X								X	X				X			X	
Arthur Middleton		X	X	X								X							X	
Bisbee															X				X	
Burlington																		X	X	
Buttonwood																			X	
Callaway		X	X				X				X							X	X	
Cambria		X	X	X							X	X	X						X	
Cor Caroli																				
Carson City																		X	X	
Cavalier											X		X						X	
Centaurus		X	X	X				X			X	X				X			X	
Coronado						X		X		X					X			X		
El Paso								X	X					X				X		
Etamin						X		X												
Eugene															X				X	
Gallup															X				X	
Glendale						X		X							X	X			X	
Hutchinson																				
Leonard Wood		X	X	X							X						X		X	
Long Beach						X		X										X		
Muskogee																			X	
Ogden								X	X											
Orange														X						
San Pedro						X		X		X				X	X			X	X	
Spencer																			X	
Sterope												X								
Tupelo												X								
Van Buren								X	X	X						X				
Woodbine											X									
FS-367																				X
LST-18						X		X	X	X				X	X		X			
LST-19											X		X			X				
LST-20																				
LST-22	X					X		X	X	X				X	X		X		X	
LST-23		X	X		X						X		X		X					
LST-24												X								
LST-26								X	X	X				X	X			X	X	
LST-66	X							X	X	X				X	X			X	X	
LST-67	X					X		X	X	X				X	X			X	X	
LST-68	X					X		X		X				X	X			X	X	
LST-70					X						X	X								
LST-71												X								
LST-166					X						X									
LST-168	X					X					X							X	X	
LST-169	X					X					X							X	X	
LST-170	X					X		X	X	X					X			X	X	
LST-201								X												
LST-202	X					X		X	X					X	X			X	X	
LST-204	X							X		X				X	X			X	X	
LST-205										X	X							X	X	
LST-206	X					X		X	X	X					X			X	X	
LST-207					X						X								X	

USS San Pedro (PF 37), Long Beach Harbor, October 1943.

26c

Official U.S. Coast Guard photo, USS Long Beach (PF-34)
Identified in other sources as San Pedro (PF-37) or Albuquerque (PF-7)

26d

The Consolidated Steel-built USS Burlington *(PF-51) seen in San Francisco Bay on 16 February 1945 during a brief underway period (1319 to 1615) to compensate compasses.* Official USN Photograph, (Hunters Point?) No. 1110-45-S4, (a copy is Naval Historical Center NH82144). Burlington *departed Bay waters on the 18th for a direct transit to Dutch Harbor, Alaska, arriving there the 26th.*

PF 46 USS BISBEE

USS Bisbee *(PF-46) underway in San Pedro Bay (Los Angeles), Calif., on 23 May 1944.* Official USN Photograph (National Archives) 19-N-66006 (other views in this series are 80-G-66004 through 66008). Bisbee *was underway on the 23rd from 0751 through 1330, conducting ten speed trial runs on the measured mile commencing at 0924.*

26e

USS Gallup *(PF-47) underway in San Pedro Bay on 30 May 1944.* Official USN Photograph. Gallup *was underway on the 30th from 0858 to about 1600, conducting speed trials during 0957 to 1345 and general quarters and fire drills subsequently until 1433. Departing San Pedro the next day,* Gallup *proceeded in company with* Bisbee *(guide and officer-in-tactical command aboard) and* Corpus Christi *(PF-44) directly to Noumea, New Caledonia, for subsequent southwestern Pacific duty.*

The Froemming-built USS Allentown *(PF-52) at Norfolk Navy Yard on 9 Aug. 1944, wearing Measure 32/16D camouflage.* Official USN Photograph 19-N-72013. *Note the HF/DF antenna aft.* Allentown *was underway from 0742 through 1840 on the 9th for main engine power trials in Chesapeake Bay, following the dismantling and "reassembly" of the main engines at Norfolk NY. Sonar gear was installed and CIC rearranged during the same time.*

26f

USS *Muskogee* (PF-49)
A Radioman, A Fireman
A Seaman & A Gunner's mate

A Pharmacist's Mate 1st Class,
Hollandia, New Guinea 1944,
and 50 years later at PF-49
reunion, 1994.

Where's the beer? First a game of baseball! A gang from San Pedro (PF-37) on the beach at Hollandia, New Guinea, April 1944.

Liberty in Cairns, Australia, 1944

26h

Would you sail with a crew like this?
USS *Eugene* (PF-40)

261

USS HUTCHINSON (PF-45)

HERE and THERE

COMMANDER JACK DEMPSEY VISITS THE "HUTCH"

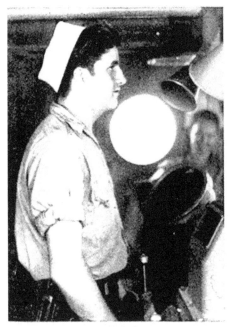

AT THE HELM

THAT 'ROO HUNT

The Wardroom Gang --- USS *Sandusky* (PF-54)

26k

MESSAGE TO THE CREW FROM THE COMMANDING OFFICER

I am proud and honored to be selected as the Commanding Officer of the U.S.S SANDUSKY. I am equally proud of the record which you officers and men have made in the training program you have just completed. In the expert opinion of those who have attended the trials of this ship, the SANDUSKY is by far the best frigate yet to be commissioned in the New Orleans area. It is fitting, therefore, that you be so assigned.

The Navy Department has spared no expense or material in the proper completion of your training. In the same token, no expense has been spared to give us a ship fully equipped to carry out the mission for which she was designed. The Navy, the builders, and the outfitting yard have completed their work. We, the officers and crew, now have our work to do. It will be necessary for us to use to the fullest extent all our training, our intelligence, and our equipment against our enemies in order to make the SANDUSKY worthy of her name and worthy of the trust that our nation has placed in us.

I wish to emphasize as fully as possible that every single officer and man has a job to perform. If he carries out that job to the best of his ability, we have nothing to fear. The life of this ship and the destiny of our country depends wholly on cooperation and unity. Forget your prejuicdes and arguments—we have a common end toward which to fight. Let us make the SANDUSKY a ship of which the Navy, the Coast Guard, the City of Sandusky, Ohio, and the whole United States is justly proud. May we have good hunting.

—T. R. SARGENT, III

MESSAGE TO THE CREW FROM THE EXECUTIVE OFFICER

The prospective crew of the prospective U.S.S SANDUSKY now becomes the first regular crew of the proud U.S.S. SANDUSKY. This crew with its long series of "bests" in the training period—best PF crew to be trained at the Naval Operatin Base, Norfolk, in the words of the training officer there; best in barracks inspection at Norfolk many times; best communications gang at Norfolk; two times winner of the flag at Manhattan Beach for the coveted "48" in New York—to enumerate a few "bests", now becomes the best blue blood that can be poured into the veins of a new ship.

The frames, plates, mast and riggings which constitute the U.S.S. SANDUSKY can boast of some "bests" in her own right. She came down ther river in the best shape of any PF to complete the journey and she is being commissioned in the best time that any frigate has achieved to date.

The ship is ready and the crew is right. It is my opinion, in which I am unanimously supported by the rest of the Wardroom, that such an intermarriage of superlatives cannot help but produce a "best" among combatant units. This, let us set as our goal forward from this commissioning day and resolve never to be content with less than the "best."

—B. M. CHISWELL, JR.

U. S. S. SANDUSKY

26L

From the latest revised edition of Volume A, DICTIONARY OF AMERICAN NAVAL FIGHTING SHIPS:

. . . On 13 November 1944 *Ardent* (AM-340) and frigate *Rockford* (PF-48) were escorting a six-ship convoy midway between Honolulu and the United States. At 1232 *Ardent's* sonar picked up a submarine contact. *Ardent* attacked first at 1241, firing a 24-charge "hedgehog" pattern. *Rockford* left her escort station to assist, and fired her first barrage of rockets from her "hedgehog" at 1308; two explosions followed before an underwater detonation rocked the ship. *Ardent* carried out two more attacks and the frigate dropped 13 depth charges to administer the coup de grace. Wreckage recovered on scene - wooden slat with Japanese writing, pieces of varnished mahogany inscribed in Japanese, deck planking containing Japanese builders inscription - indicated a definite "kill." Postwar research revealed the sunken submarine to be the Japanese *I-12*, which had sailed from the Inland Sea on 4 October 1944 to disrupt American shipping between the West Coast and the Hawaiian Islands. In sinking *I-12*, *Ardent* and *Rockford* unwittingly avenged the atrocity *I-12* had perpetrated on 30 October when, after sinking the Liberty ship *John A. Johnson*, the submarine had rammed and sunk the lifeboats and rafts and then machine-gunned the 70 survivors. . .

USS *Rockford* (PF-48) underway in northern waters, wearing "disruptive" camouflage designed to confuse an enemy observer as to the ship's course.

A Sea Story from Dale Benson

The *Rockford* had sailed from Long Beach, California, to Cairns, Australia, and then on to New Guinea where we took on 206 cases of beer - - - about one case per sailor. Unfortunately, when the final count was taken in the ship's commissary, there were only 200 cases accounted for. Our extremely astute, respected and sea-wise captain, Cmdr. David A Bartlett, came on the PA with, "Now here this! Today we took on 206 cases of beer. At this time, there are 200 cases accounted for in the commissary. Tomorrow morning by 0800, there will be 206 cases of beer in the commissary. Failing this, I will form a work detail and will throw 200 cases overboard." There was no need for a work detail at 0800 the following morning.

26m

UNITED STATES FLEET
COMMANDER SEVENTH FLEET

By virtue of the power delegated to me, I take
pleasure in awarding in the name of the President of the United States,
the Bronze Star Medal to:

LIEUTENANT F. J. HELIGER
U.S. COAST GUARD RESERVE

CITATION

For distinguishing himself by heroic achievement
in leading a salvage party aboard the S.S. Saugraine which had been
abandoned after being twice torpedoed by aircraft on 5 December 1944. He
personally inspected every compartment of the damaged vessel, despite
recurrent enemy air attacks, to determine the extent of damage. His accurate report enabled the Senior Officer Present Afloat to reverse his
previous decision to sink the vessel, and to decide to attempt to salvage her. His assistance in rescuing over two hundred Army survivors
from the above vessel was outstanding. His conduct throughout has distinguished him among those performing duties of the same character.

D. L. BARBEY,
Vice Admiral, U. S. Navy,
Commander Seventh Fleet.

Bronze Star awarded to Lt. Heliger while serving aboard USS *San Pedro* (PF-37). Select crewmen
boarded the *Saugraine* along with Lt. Heliger to assist in inspection of compartments and
preparation of damage report.

26n

MEMORIES OF SHIPMATES ABOARD THE USS OGDEN, PF-39
IN THE SOUTH PACIFIC DURING WORLD WAR II

SFC Jim Feeney: I think he was from Philadelphia; well liked by all who knew him. He was a member of the 3'50 gun crew when a round failed to clear the breech and fell in the gun tub. Feeney grabbed the live shell and hurled it over the side. We always thought that was a brave thing to do, but nothing much was said about it.

Jim was also the center of a near free-for-all. A Navy ship pulled alongside the Ogden one day and as was the custom, attempted to tie-up. Lines were thrown across with a leaded "monkey fist" to give it weight. Procedure called for the thrower to shout a warning, but this never happened. Feeney was on deck watch with an M-1 rifle and the "monkey fist" struck him in the head, opening up an ugly cut. Since there never was much love lost between the Coast Guard and Navy, only quick reaction by officers and CPOs kept a number of Ogden shipmates from boarding the Navy destroyer and starting a real donnybrook.

Lt. Cdr. Kemp Niver of San Diego; executive officer: He'll always be remembered for the famous words, "Beer For All Hands." His voice boomed over the loudspeaker after the Ogden was credited for downing three Jap planes in Leyte Gulf. Niver was normally spit and polish. When the gun crews made their first kill, he admonished the cheering crew to cease and retain their readiness. At the all clear, he was joined by Captain Kenneth Tharp of Lomita, California, in congratulating the crew.

Quartermaster Earl Rippee, Newport Beach, California: Earl will never forget the convoy that included an Australian merchant ship from New Guinea to Leyte. Enroute, a Japanese torpedo plane dove toward the Australian ship but had to go over the Ogden to reach it. Earl's secondary assignment was a 50 cal. machine gun to primarily "repel boarders". With all anti-aircraft guns on the Ogden firing, Earl turned the machine gun toward the torpedo plane and still remembers seeing that torpedo aimed "straight between my legs!" The Ogden's crew provided a happy ending, the plane was hit and cart-wheeled over the Australian ship which signaled the Ogden a message that loosely said "well done mates".

All ships in combat were given code names for ship to ship and ship to shore radio messages. The Ogden answered to the name of Carstairs. Two particular messages keep coming to mind--"Carstairs, get away from that cow!" This was transmitted while we were in Leyte Gulf and apparently heading for a tanker for fuel when it was not quite secure enough. Tankers were a prime target for Kamikazes. Then another comes to mind--"Carstairs, Carstairs, do you have any whole blood?!" Who called and why, I never found out.

The most memorable radio message--"Flash red, control yellow, many bogies!" translated, this meant an air raid with Japanese in control of the skies. Luckily, it wasn't long before we heard--"Flash red, control green!" Our planes had control and we were to stop firing.

Dick Brady Rm2/c

David Hendrickson

260

SOMEWHERE IN THE PACIFIC

I am somewhere in the Pacific
Where the sun is like a curse.
And each scorching day is followed
By another one slightly worse.

Where the dust blows thicker
Than the ever shifting sand,
Where all the sailors dream and wish
For fair and better land.

We are somewhere in the Pacific
Where a woman is never seen;
Where the sky is never cloudy
And the grass is always green.

Where the planes are flying nightly,
Robs a man of blessed sleep;
Where there isn't any whiskey, and
The word "Beer" makes you weep.

Somewhere in the Pacific
There the nights are made for love,
And the moon is like a searchlight
With the Southern Cross above.

Stars shine like a diamond cluster
In a balmy tropic night,
It's a shameless waste of beauty
And not a girl in sight.

Somewhere in the Pacific
There the mail is always late,
A christmas card in April
Is considered up to date.

Somewhere in the Pacific
Where the ants and lizards play,
And there's a million flies
To replace every one you slay.

Where we never have a pay
And we never spend a cent;
But we never miss the money
Cause it just can't be spent.

I'm somewhere in the Pacific
But the place I cannot tell
It's really not a country
Just a substitute for HELL

From the scrap book of W. I. Westmoreland, Lt.(jg)
USS Eugene (PF-40) - Passed Over The Bar

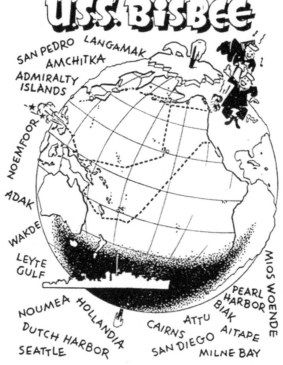

26p

A "typical"

frigate cruise

of WWII

15 February, 1944—Commissioned at Terminal Island, California.

1 April, 1944—Arrived San Diego, California, commenced shakedown cruise.

29 April, 1944—Completed shakedown cruise. Arrived San Pedro, California.

31 May, 1944—1700 anchors aweigh. The *Bisbee* is off to join the fight in the Southwest Pacific.

11 June, 1944—Crossed the equator. Two hundred five Pollywogs became Shellbacks.

18 June, 1944—Crossed the International Date Line from West Longitude into the mysterious East, Domain of the Golden Dragon.

21 June, 1944—First foreign port: Noumea, New Caledonia.

24 June, 1944—Across the Coral Sea, through the Great Barrier Reef.

28 June, 1944—Cairns, Australia.

6 July, 1944—North to Papua, through the China Straits to Milne Bay, New Guinea.

13 July, 1944—Through the Goshen Straits, up the north coast of New Guinea in the Bismark Sea past Buna, Lae, Langamak and Aitape to Hollandia, Netherlands West Indies.

17 July, 1944—Humboldt Bay. Began trading with natives.

22 July, 1944—On up the north coast of New Guinea to Wakde, past the Padaido Islands to Biak in the Shoutens. This was the forward area. Here was our job.

7 August, 1944—Bombarded the village of Wardo at the mouth of the Napidori River on the west coast of Biak. Farther west in the Geelvink Bay, from loyal Dutch natives on Rani and Insobabi Islands. collected seven Japanese prisoners of war.

17 August, 1944—Bombarded enemy gun emplacements near the mouth of the Napadori River on the west coast of Biak, supporting landing of elements of the 41st Infantry Division.

25 August, 1944—Bombarded enemy positions in the vicinity of Oboebari on the north coast of Biak, supporting landing of elements of the 41st Infantry Division.

11 September, 1944—Rescued injured Australian pilot in the waters of Geelvink Bay west of Noemfoor Island.

19 September, 1944—Seadler Harbor, Admiralty Islands.

12 October, 1944—North across the Equator again, past the Palaus, across the Mindanao deep to Leyte Gulf, Philippine Islands.

18 October, 1944—Bombarded enemy positions on the south coast of Homonhon Island at the entrance of Leyte Gulf in support of landings made by U. S. Rangers who completed liberation of the first of the Philippine Islands on that day.

19 October, 1944—From position in the entrance of Leyte Gulf served as Harbor Entrance Control Post guiding hundreds of ships safely into Leyte Gulf through the mined waters of Surigao Strait.

19 October, 1944—Drove off the first attacking enemy plane with our gunfire.

25 October, 1944—Observed the Battle of Surigao Strait from a position thirteen miles to the northeast in which old battleships of the Seventh Fleet completely demolished the Japanese force of two battleships, four cruisers, and ten destroyers.

25 October, 1944—At 0555 a torpedo from a Japanese Betty bomber passed thirty feet under our stern. Manned all battle stations continuously for the next six days. On 5 November and 21 November anchored in San Pedro Bay, near Tacloban, Leyte.

20 November, 1944—Relieved of duties as Harbor Entrance Control for Leyte Gulf.

22 November, 1944—Departed Philippine area after 34 days for Humboldt Bay again, then east to Manus Island, north and east between the Gilberts and the Marshals to Oahu, Hawaii.

15 December, 1944—Arrived Pearl Harbor and the Royal Hawaiian Hotel.

6 January, 1945—North to the Aleutians. Through Unimak Pass into the Bering Sea.

6 July, 1945—Homeward Bound.

11 July, 1945—Landfall again: Vancouver Island, British Columbia, Canada, and the Olympic Peninsula, Washington, U. S. A.

CHAPTER 3

Tales of the North Pacific

Of the twelve frigates built by Kaiser Cargo Company at Richmond on San Francisco Bay, not one ventured any closer to the tropics than San Diego on the 32nd parallel North during wartime service. From the cool waters of the West Coast to the cold waters of the Gulf of Alaska and the Bering Sea, the Kaiser frigates escaped the below decks stifling conditions that plagued the frigates of the Seventh Fleet in the Southwest Pacific. En route to decommissioning in the spring of 1946, *Grand Island, Pueblo, Casper,* and *Grand Forks* did experience the tropics briefly while navigating the Panama Canal on their way to Charleston, South Carolina, where they were laid up to await the scrap pile or sale to foreign nations. *Grand Forks* and *Casper* were scrapped. *Grand Island* went to Cuba as the *Maximo Gomez* and *Pueblo* joined the Dominican Navy in 1948 as the *Presidente Peynado,* later renamed *Cap. General Pedro Santana. Pocatello* and *Brownsville,* decommissioned on the West Coast in 1946, along with the above four made up the war years contingent assigned to Western Sea Frontier engaged in weather patrol and plane guard duty out of San Diego, San Francisco and Seattle. One interesting feature of the two-year careers of these frigates was that whether planned or not, they appeared to serve as training ships for commanding officers. In less than two years' time, *Pueblo* piped aboard five commanding officers, *Brownsville* four, *Pocatello, Grand Forks* and *Grand Island* three each and *Casper* two.

Launched on 17 October 1943, *Pocatello* had the honor of being sponsored by the great-granddaughter of Chief Pocatello who had gained prominence in western railroad building and remembered by the city of the same name in Idaho. During the war years, *Pocatello* was the only West Coast frigate to spend her entire career on weather duty. She worked out of Seattle alternating with the old 240 ft cutter *Haida* on Station Able, 49 degrees N latitude -149 degrees W Longitude or about 1,500 miles west of Seattle and 500 miles south of Kodiak in the Gulf of Alaska. In the course of her assignment, the frigate completed a dozen patrols, the sequence consisting of thirty days at sea followed by ten days in Seattle. She did enjoy one lengthy reprieve in the winter of 1944 when *Casper* showed up for a month of heavy weather relief patrolling. In an anniversary letter to the crew of *Casper,* commanding officer Scheiber noted:

> ....Remember, then, we went north, and some of you discovered that you were not as salty as you wished others to believe you were. That cruise showed you that the *Casper* could take it, and that you could take whatever she dished out. We didn't encounter much "shipping over weather" on that cruise; instead, it was weather that obviously would separate the men from the boys. It was rugged for a few weeks and then we

came back home...

Pueblo, Casper, Grand Island and *Grand Forks* worked weather patrol and plane guard out of San Francisco on a usual schedule of three weeks at sea and two weeks in port.

27a

USS *Grand Forks* (PF-11)

27b

NATIONAL AIR TRANSPORT SERVICE

Air Transport Squadron Two

U. S. Naval Air Station

VR-2/P15   Alameda, California

Serial: 0185   6 Nov. 1944

R E S T R I C T E D

From: Commander, Air Transport Squadron TWO.
To :   Commander, Western Sea Frontier
Via :   Commander, Naval Air Transport Service, Pacific.

Subject: USS GRAND FORKS - Commendation of.

1.   This command wishes to commend the officers and men of the USS GRAND FORKS for their excellent cooperation in connection with the recent forced landing of PB2Y-5R aircraft, Bureau Number 7221.

2.   By intelligent use of the experience, knowledge and equipment at their disposal the USS GRAND FORKS circumvented unfavorable conditions and, with the use of searchlights and flares, aided the pilot materially in making a safe landing. Also the outstanding manner in which the plane's crew members, passengers and cargo were transferred to the USS GRAND FORKS under difficult conditions of high seas, is worthy of the highest praise from this command.

3.   The consideration shown to the crew members and passengers while aboard the USS GRAND FORKS for seven days is likewise deeply appreciated by this command.

/s/   W. M. NATION

PRAIRIE PIONEER PRESS

VOL. 24, NO. 2   STUHR MUSEUM   FEBRUARY, 1990

World War II Patrol Frigate Carried Landlocked City's Name to Sea

The U.S.S. Grand Island (PF-14), man-of-war of the United States Navy, is under steam and looking for a fight, 1944. (U.S. Navy Photo, National Archives)

From a letter to the crew of *Grand Island* from former commanding officer, Lt. Cmdr. Harry Morgan upon his inability to attend the 1992 PFRA reunion at Colorado Springs.

. . . Several incidents are still fresh in my mind. I recall the sideboys and honors accorded an admiral in the Bay area. - and our anti-brass ship's mascot, Scupper, biting his hand when he tried to befriend it! Another took place at the Navy yard in San Diego. We were easing into a berth prior to repairs and I rang up 1/3 astern - got 1/3 ahead instead. - jangled the telegraph, rang up 2/3 astern - still faster ahead - finally full astern - crash! The bow split a steam line at the end of the slip and got the commodore's attention. The chief engineer never admitted to wrong bells, but we did miss some submarines close aboard. Those of you who made our Dec-Jan patrol off the Aleutians will never under-estimate the forces of nature. I think we made some Christians on that patrol, and proved that the patrol frigate was a very seaworthy design.

Brownsville worked out of San Diego until late in the war when she joined the Northern Sector in San Francisco. Assigned to West Coast Sound School at San Diego she was underway every Monday morning with whatever array of ships had assembled for shakedown exercises. One exercise included the new battleship *North Carolina, Brownsville* steaming at 18 knots in the van of ships 1,000 yards ahead of the battleship. *North Carolina* hoisted flags indicating increase of speed to 28 knots and as soon as all ships acknowledged "execute," *Brownsville* increased speed to maximum 20 knots. The OOD rang for the CO who was not located for several minutes. With *North Carolina* closing fast, 800 yards, 500 yards, 200 yards, the OOD on his own authority ordered right rudder at which moment the CO appeared and noting the breaking of the line ordered 'left full rudder.' *Brownsville* veered across the bow of the battleship, the near miss sworn to by panic stricken deck hands at less than 100 feet. Later in the day *Brownsville* was assigned a new station at the trailing end of the van. The frigate redeemed her honor working out of San Francisco on plane guard, when in the dead of night a B-29, enroute from Hawaii radioed engine failure. *Brownsville* laid a string of flares oriented in a direction best suited for ditching. Several miles short of the flares the aircraft lost its last engine and went into the sea. Fifteen survivors and three bodies were recovered and delivered to San Francisco.

On patrol in October 1944, *Grand Forks* picked up a distress call late in the night of the 11th from a PB2Y about to make an emergency landing in a sea where the swells were running up to six feet. Racing to the location and firing off flares and star shells, *Grand Forks* guided the aircraft to a safe landing and successfully rescued fifteen crewmen and passengers as well as 114 sacks of mail.

War in the North Pacific and the Bering Sea had little influence on the outcome of World War II, and even though early in the war the Japanese saw the Aleutians "pointing like a dagger at the heart of Japan," naval historian Samuel Eliot Morison had it right when he wrote: "... No operations in this region of almost perpetual mist and snow accomplished anything of importance... It was a theater of military frustrations. Both sides would have done well to leave the Aleutians to the few Aleuts unfortunate enough to live there..." However, as part of the Midway offensive, the Japanese had occupied Attu and Kiska at the western end of the chain, and as such, the Americans were obliged to retake these US owned islands. The Navy went to work in the spring of 1943 to regain the islands. First success was the Battle of the Komandorskis, fought south of the Russian islands located about halfway between Attu and Kamchatka. Admiral Hosogaya with a superior fleet escorting reinforcements to Attu was attacked by the two cruisers, *Salt Lake City* and *Richmond* and four destroyers under Admiral "Soc" McMorris. During long range exchanges, *Salt Lake City,* nicknamed "Old Swayback Maru," went dead in the water, quickly hidden by a smokescreen laid down by *Richmond.* McMorris ordered his destroyers to deliver a torpedo attack on the fast-approaching enemy.

Five minutes into the chase by destroyers Coghlan, Bailey and Monaghan, Hosogaya broke off the engagement, turning west on a heading for Japan. 11 May 1943, American forces landed on Attu, securing the island by the end of the month following a bloody affair of heavy casualties on both sides. Kiska was invaded in July only to find that the Japanese had slipped away in the fog. As Morison put it, "During the rest of the war the Aleutians offer little of interest. Harassing raids on Paramushiro were varied by occasional shore bombardments and feeble Japanese retaliatory raids on Attu, Kiska and Adak. .. In any case, it was wonderful practice ground for armed forces; after a tour of duty in the Aleutians, every other field of action seemed good." The Mountain Training Group of the 10th Mountain Infantry was sent to Dutch Harbor and Adak to learn their trade in the worst of weather. Task Force 94, variously made up of the old four-stacker cruisers *Raleigh*, *Richmond*, *Detroit* and *Concord* and accompanying destroyers swung at anchor in Kuluk Bay, Adak, between periodic bombardment of Paramushiro and Matsuwa in the Japanese Kurils across the Bering Sea. In the worst of flying conditions the Eleventh Air Force and Navy Air Wing Four carried out in excess of 1,500 sorties by war's end from Adak and Attu against the Kuril bases.

With the Japanese gone and the Aleutians secured, the Joint Chiefs abandoned any thought of an invasion of the Kurils 650 miles from the western Aleutians, partly because of the eternal hostile weather that both sides knew as the common enemy. The Aleuts called the Aleutians the "Birthplace of bad weather"--wind, rain, snow, sleet, fog, clouds and storms. The great arc of the Aleutian chain forms the battle front where moist, unstable Pacific air warmed by the subtropical Kuroshio (Japan) Current clashes with cold, dry Siberian air sweeping south across the chilled Bering Sea. The Kuroshio Current, a counterpart of the Gulf Stream in the Atlantic, keeps Aleutian waters ice-free and warm enough to influence rapid evaporation, water vapor rising aloft to condense into unbroken cloud cover. The Aleutians enjoy no calm or dry season and no station records more than ten clear days a year. Shemya, for instance, near Attu at the end of the chain, suffers a July average cloud cover of thirty days with twenty-four days of dense fog. Shemya has experienced winds of an estimated 139 mph, and in any case, winds in excess of 50 mph and the infamous Aleutian williwaws that drive rain, sleet and fog at speeds up to 100 mph, are common most of the year, less known during the brief summer. Summer in the Aleutians is a time of dense fogs that roam the Bering Sea from Unimak Pass to Attu, fogs so persistent that summer storms fail to disperse them.

General Simon B. Buckner of Alaska Defense Command early in the war wrote, "The Naval officer had an instinctive dread of Aleutian waters, feeling that they were inhabited by a ferocious monster that was always breathing fog and coughing up williwaws that would blow the unfortunate mariner onto uncharted rocks and forever destroy his chances of becoming an admiral." After the Battle of the Komandorskis and the Attu campaign, Admiral

King stated, "That chain of islands provides as rugged a theater for warfare as any in the world. Not only are islands mountainous and rocky, but the weather in the western part is continuously bad. The fogs are almost continuous and thick. Violent winds with accompanying heavy seas make any kind of operation in that vicinity difficult and uncertain." An Air Force spokesman recorded, "It can be said that no American of World War II served on a front that continuously tested both mental and physical fiber as did the cold, gray, wind-lashed, unforgiving Aleutians."

In this hostile environment the Coast Guard had known a long and honored tradition. By the 1890s the Bering Sea Patrol of the Revenue Cutter Service had earned the respect of smugglers and the welcome of ice-locked native villages. Of all the turn of the century cutters in the Bering Sea, a long-time stalwart, the *Bear,* earned lasting honors. Later under the Coast Guard, created by act of Congress in 1915 by combining the Revenue Cutter Service and the Life-Saving Service, the 240 ft. cutter *Haida,* launched in 1921, joined the Bering Sea Patrol and stayed on for twenty years. *Haida* was pressed into escort duty and antisubmarine patrol in the Bering Sea when war broke out, duties that ended in 1943, only months before CortDiv 27 made up of Kaiser frigates 3,4,5,6,7 and 8 began appearing one-by-one to take up similar tasks.

CortDiv 14 made up of destroyer escorts *Engstrom, Austin, Doherty* and *Doneff* set course for the Aleutians in September 1943, and following a winter of escort and patrol eagerly awaited arrival of CortDiv 27 for relief to come by late spring 1944. But expectation turned to disappointment when only frigates *Albuquerque* and *Everett* arrived on schedule in April. Protracted post-shakedown availability delayed arrival of *Hoquiam* until 27 August, *Sausalito* until 5 October, *Pasco* until 15 October and lastly, troubled-plagued *Tacoma* avoided the Bering Sea until 21 October. As a result of CortDiv 27 tardiness, Engstrom, the last of CortDiv 14, lingered in the Aleutians until January 1945, a lengthy tour just short of fifteen months. At the end of her tour in June 1945, *Albuquerque* was not far behind at fourteen months and *Everett* nearby at thirteen and one-half months.

As noted by former SK1/c and plank owner Earl Day, the *Tacoma* represented the prime example of Kaiser frigates subject to post-construction and post-shakedown problems:

> After completing shakedown training off the California coast in December 1943, *Tacoma* reported for duty as a training ship in January 1944. She trained prospective frigate crews until 27 June, when she was ordered to proceed to Alaskan waters upon completion of sea trials. However, she was plagued by unsuccessful trials due to a seemingly constant problem with hot bearings. Being the first of her class it appeared future frigates benefitted from mechanical failures of the *Tacoma.* In addition a boiler room fire, resulting in the death of a shipmate, delayed

Tacoma from reporting for duty at Kodiak until 21 October 1944. For the next four months, as a member of Escort Division 27, *Tacoma* conducted antisubmarine and other patrols and escorted supply vessels and transports along the Alaskan coast and between the various islands of the Aleutian chain, visiting Atlu, Adak, Dutch Harbor until the bearing problem arose again resulting in her leaving Dutch Harbor on 23 February 1945, for an extensive overhaul, first in San Francisco, then to Bremerton, Washington, to prepare her for transfer to the Soviet Union.

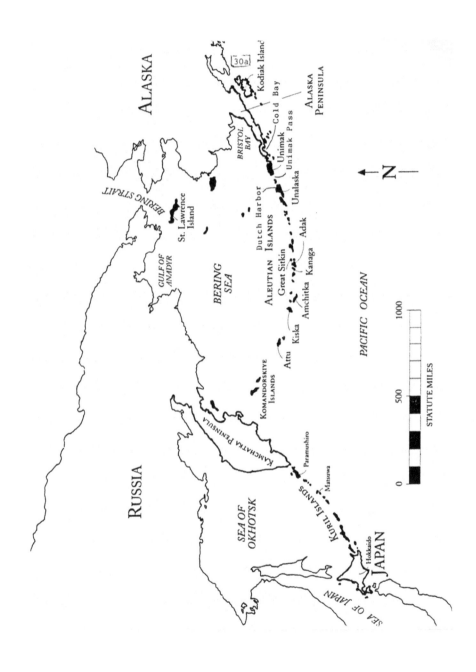

30b

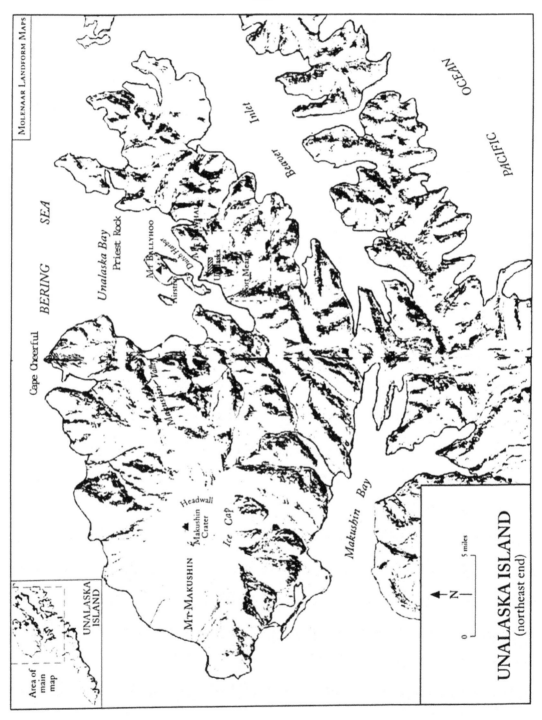

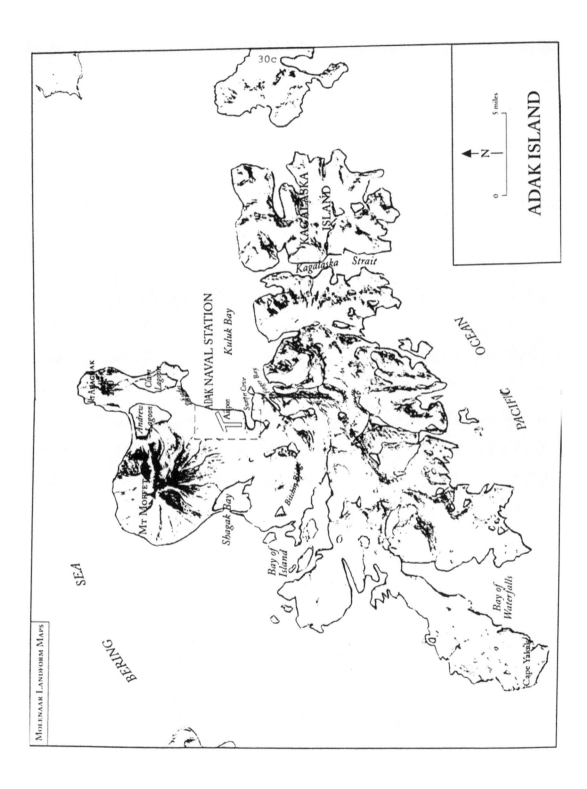

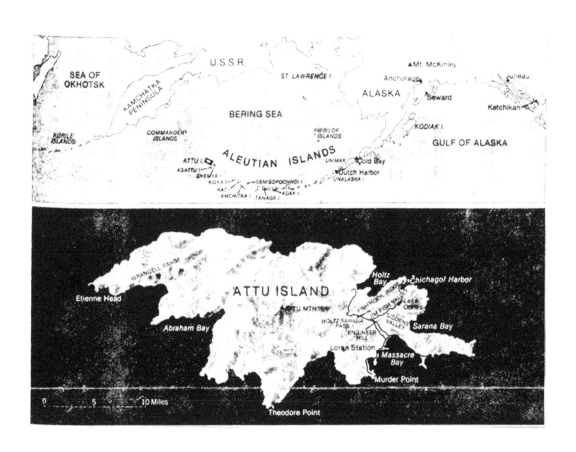

Attu from Massacre Bay

30e

Detail aft aboard USS Albuquerque (PF-7), seen at Pier 23 Mare Island Navy Yard on 20 March 1944. **Official USN Photograph, Mare Island No. 1821-44.** *Albuquerque was underway in San Francisco Bay the 21st and 23rd preparatory to departing the 26th for Seattle, Wa., after a brief stay at MINY.*

30f

One of the first Tacoma (PF-3) class ships, the Kaiser-built Hoquiam (PF-5) moored to Pier 23 North, Mare Island Navy Yard on 14 June 1944. Official USN Photograph, Mare Island No. 3567-44. Visible recent alterations forward are highlighted in white. Hoquiam was visited by a senior "naval inspecting party" led by RADM Hugh Noyes USN from 0915 through 1200 this day.

On 11 April 1944, six days out of Seattle, Scotch Cap light. guarding Unimak Pass arose to starboard at *0315,* announcing *Albuquerque's* arrival in the bleak and barren Aleutian Islands and authorizing entrance into the Bering Sea and passage to nearby Dutch Harbor. Eleven days later *Everett* completed a similar passage across the North Pacific to drop her hook in Sweeper Cove, Adak, midway along the Aleutian chain. Unlike the Seventh Fleet frigates, these two failed to meet or work together for months, each engaged in what they would discover was a war of loneliness. Single ship patrols, single ship responses to distress calls, convoys of as few as one or two vessels and never more than two zigzagging escorts, and more often than not an overwhelming feeling of isolation accentuated by the enclosing qualities of ever-enduring bad weather.

Albuquerque cleared Unimak Pass as dawn broke, Unimak Island to starboard and Akun Island to port, slopes clothed in lasting winter snow, upper reaches lost in stratus clouds and a rocky and unfriendly shoreline lapped by gray seas reflecting unbroken gray skies. Bearing to port the frigate bore down on Cape Cheerful and the gulf-wide entrance to Unalaska Bay leading to protected Dutch Harbor. Grim and barren Cape Cheerful inspires little cheer, perhaps a misnomer decreed by the same Jack London who bestowed the fanciful name of Mt. Ballyhoo to the peak overhanging Dutch Harbor on little Amaknak Island. In any case though, Cape Cheerful does point the way into the finest landlocked harbor in the Aleutians. Only Adak and Kiska offer similar safe harbors. Constantine Harbor at Amchitka, Alcan Cove at Shemya and Massacre Bay at Attu are little more than open roadsteads requiring ships to anchor away from docks in heavy weather.

Entering Dutch Harbor for the first time, PF-7 slipped by brooding Priest Rock to port, ever watchful of all those who dared a last look when homeward bound with the promise of return to the Bering Sea. To starboard of the channel, which separated Amaknak Island from Unalaska Island, a low sandy spit melted away about a mile inland at Spithead light. Across the spit in protected Iliuliuk Bay, Ballyhoo Dock and Advanced Base Dock (ABD) could be made out at the foot of snow-draped Mt. Ballyhoo. The naval air strip dipped into Iliuliuk Bay between the shadow of Mt. Ballyhoo and the huddled buildings of Navy Town and Navy Operating Base (NOB) tower. Beyond view on the far side of Amaknak Island a cable ferry led to Unalaska Village strung out along a sloping rocky beach.

Albuquerque rounded Spithead light to moor alongside USS *Wickes* DD-578 at Dutch Harbor Dock adjacent to Navy Town. From a diving barge, a diver descended to inspect bilge keels and found twelve feet of keel broken away from its welding and turned back against the ship's bottom, the breakaway occurring during heavy weather enroute to Dutch Harbor. The loose section was cut away in time for departure at 1830 with a convoy bound for the Gulf of Alaska. So within hours of arrival PF-7 was outbound in a rising sea on her first assignment, making for Unimak Pass as gale force winds and a slashing rain assailed the line of ships in search of Scotch Cap light and safe passage to a prearranged convoy separation point. At departure the log entry read:

> "... Unmoored and standing out of Dutch Harbor with convoy formed up in the following manner--SS TURIALBA in position 11 (convoy guide), USAT WILLIAM L THOMPSON position 21, SS HENDERSON LUELLING position 31, SS CHIEF WASHAKIE position 12, SS WILLIAM T. SHERMAN position 22 in accordance with U.S. Naval Op. Base, Dutch Harbor, confidential orders, this vessel steering courses at all engines ahead standard speed 135 rpm, zigzagging patrol station ahead of convoy. 2000-2400 maintain convoy speed 10 knots."

Albuquerque departed the convoy three days steaming time east of Unimak Pass for return to Dutch Harbor late on the 16th. Following a brief two day rest, lights flashed on at 0427 on the 19th as the PA blared orders to set special sea detail, the announced mission to render assistance to the distressed Liberty ship *John W Straub,* reported sinking twenty-one miles off Sanak Island near Cold Bay, 200 miles distance. So once again PF-7 made for Unimak Pass. Scotch Cap light passed to port as SS *Taloa,* heading west, blinkered a cryptic message: "We have no survivors of *Straub* aboard." Under gray skies and a slight sea, the frigate cranked up to near flank speed of 20 knots. At exactly high noon the port side sky lookout called out a sighting, within minutes identified as the stern section of the ill-fated *Straub.* Battle stations sounded, bringing gun crews on deck to join watch lookouts in visual search for survivors and bodies.

Through scattered dunnage and lumber, several life rafts, one capsized boat and countless fifty-gallon oil drums, the frigate worked in close to the derelict. No survivors or bodies were sighted. It was later learned that the freighter carried 8,000 drums of aviation gasoline and 25,000 drums of diesel fuel bound for Attu. The remains of the *Straub,* her stern slanting skyward, rudder and propeller partly above water, was estimated at 100 feet in length and boarding was possible at a ragged section of the after main deck.

At this point a small Army boat from Fort Randall, Cold Bay, hove into view and signaled the rescue of fifteen men. *Albuquerque* then maneuvered to leeward of the wreck and lowered her whaleboat. Away from the ship for thirty minutes, the boarding party returned to report no sign of life aboard and that the Liberty ship had parted aft of the engine room bulkhead, evidence suggesting a violent explosion but no sign of fire. The fifteen survivors, including the third mate, one seaman and thirteen Navy Armed Guard crewmen, all testified that following a violent explosion the forward section sank in less than one minute. The sinking claimed the lives of the captain and four ship's officers, thirty-five merchant seamen, fourteen Navy men and the cargo security officer, fifty-five in all. Early on, the Navy believed that the sinking was the result of an internal explosion. A Coast Guard confidential report of 5 October 1944, credited the sinking to a mine, but there remained unanswered the possibility of a torpedo sinking by Japanese submarine I-180, sunk by *Gilmore* DE-18 on 26 April, less than 400 miles from the *Straub* sinking. *Albuquerque* had returned to Dutch Harbor on the 20th and moored alongside *Gilmore*. *Gilmore* departed for Kodiak with a convoy on the 23rd, identified a surfaced submarine on the 25th, gained underwater sound contact at 0010 on the 26th, dropped twelve depth charges and recorded successful sinking of the I-180.

Meanwhile back at the scene of the tragedy, late on the 19th, it was time to sink the derelict with 3-inch gunfire or work in close and fire off a K-gun depth charge. But then with a rumble of escaping air, the last of the *John* W. *Straub* slipped below the gray swells at 1550 hours, location 54° 16' N. Latitude, 163° 44' W. Longitude in 55 fathoms of water.

With no frigates in sight and *Everett* prowling somewhere in the western Aleutians, *Albuquerque* departed Dutch Harbor on 25 April in company with destroyer escort *Austin* and a convoy of five ships bound for Adak. This trip marked the beginning of routine escort duty, stretching 1,500 miles from Kodiak in the Gulf of Alaska to Attu at the end of the Aleutian chain. The short summer would come and go, seas generally no worse than moderate and fog a constant companion. Depending on the weather, the run from Dutch Harbor to Kodiak via Unimak Pass required three to four days, and west to Adak two to three days and the same from Adak to Attu at the end of the chain. From April to August *Albuquerque* escorted twenty-two convoys for a total of eighty-four days at sea in what seemed endless stop and go from Monotony to Boredom to Apathy, a.k.a. in any order, Dutch Harbor, Adak, Attu. As for liberty in the Aleutians, forget it. A trip to Kodiak was a welcome escape from the treeless tundra and muskeg of the Aleutian landscape to the wooded evergreen softness of Kodiak Island and the single unpaved main street of Kodiak lined with a sufficient number of bars and eateries. In Kodiak, section liberty began after noon chow, sailors piling into an open "cattle car" attached to a semi-tractor for the ride into town. Liberty ended at dark when the shore patrol swept the bars, often a time of sharp disagreement and invitations to brawling.

Navy Special Services provided an unlimited supply of "B" films for showing at sea and first run films borrowed on a one night basis when in port. The evening's film was usually preceded by a seriously out of date newsreel. Mess tables were laid down so that viewers could lean against table tops while seated on life jackets. Officers sat in wardroom chairs at the rear, and you knew the evening was underway when the RKO Pathe News white rooster flapped his wings and crowed to some wise guy's shout of "Latest war news, Pearl Harbor bombed!"

A break in the routine of escort duty for *Albuquerque* began late in the afternoon of Sunday, 20 August, following a welcome day of rest moored to West Navy Pier, Attu--not a particularly welcome break as it turned out. Four Navy aviation radiomen came aboard for temporary assignment as IFF (Identification Friend or Foe) experts. As dusk fell and under a dense fog, the frigate cleared Massacre Bay shaping a course for a five day Guard Ship Station patrol off the Komandorski Islands, 300 miles west of Attu. *Albuquerque* was the first frigate to participate in Guard Ship patrol, previously the province of Navy DEs. Once the rest of CortDiv 27 arrived and along with the crowd of six frigates to show up from the Southwest Pacific, this patrol became the soul responsibility of the Coast Guard-manned frigates until war's end. The weather on station was always bad and unbelievably nasty once winter set in. On her first patrol, PF-7 relieved destroyer escort *Doneff* and her tired crew that had been on an extended patrol of nearly three weeks. The patrol traced roughly a sixty mile diameter circle, on certain segments Medny Island in the Komandorskis was picked up by radar and at other times the highlands of Kamchatka showed up. The ship's responsibility called for maintaining IFF response with 11th Air Force bombers raiding in the Kurils, radar surveillance for Japanese aircraft and rescue in case an American bomber ditched.

After a few days rest back in Attu, heavy seas and high winds were pounding Massacre Bay on the 30th of August when Fleet Air Wing Four signaled *Albuquerque's* second patrol, this time for seven days to begin on the 31st. Under difficult conditions the frigate maneuvered to moor alongside fuel barge YO-163, seas washing over the barge as the frigate tossed lines to moor on her leeward side. Surging soon snapped two stern lines which fouled around the starboard propeller as swells lifted *Albuquerque's* stern to collide with deck stanchions on YO-163. The vessels surged together, protected only by thick fenders rigged between the two while waves and spray drenched the stern line crew attempting to clear the fouled propeller. Finally free, the post-refueling report stated no damage, but once underway in the open sea the engineers noted a slight noise in the starboard shaft and propeller at standard speed of 135 rpm.

The seven day patrol was one of exceptionally foul weather to the point that the mess deck saw little activity, meals deferred in favor of sandwiches and soup served in coffee mugs. West Navy Pier provided a welcome anchor of stability on 7 September. A propeller damage report submitted on the 7th stated:

> "This vessel completed a seven day patrol of 2100 miles without incident except for vibration and slight foreign noise over starboard propeller noticeable in steering engine room at standard speed. Visual inspection in clear water (7Sept) revealed all starboard propeller blades bent backward for approximately 12 inches from blade tip. Immediate inspection of starboard engine and tail shaft for possible misalignment and replacement of starboard propeller is requested."

Hopes for escape to Mare Island or Puget Sound were quickly dashed when word from Adm. Frank Jack Fletcher, Commander Alaska Sea Frontier, directed *Albuquerque* to proceed to Finger Bay, Adak, for dry-dock and replacement of the damaged screw. In an air of gloom the frigate departed Attu on 14 September, shaping a course for Adak in company with her sister *Everett* (first meeting of the two frigates since arrival in the Aleutians in April), escorting fleet oiler *Salinas* AO-18. Admiral Fletcher was good to his word, for there on the dock, on 18 September, gleaming brightly under leaden skies, a newly cast propeller awaited *Albuquerque's* needs.

34a

USS Everett (PF-8) moored alongside ARD-6, Captain's Bay, Dutch Harbor

34b

The party is underway for a gang from Everett (PF-8), Kodiak, Alaska, 30 September 1944.

All dressed up for liberty? in Dutch Harbor, Unalaska, Aleutian Islands, August 1944.

Ready to crack steam at the anchor windlass, Adak.

Hoquiam and Sausalito were on scene by early October and Pasco and Tacoma on their way north, but none were available to steam in company with Albuquerque during a violent weather episode out of Kodiak beginning on 7 October. Standing out of Women's Bay near nightfall on the 7th, in company with PCE 880 bound for Unimak Pass and Dutch Harbor, herding Liberty ship tanker John P. Altgeld and freighter Taloa, gusting winds, white caps in the channel and a rapidly tumbling barometer vouched for coming dirty weather. The life lines had been rigged by the change of the watch at 2000. Winds had risen to gale force by 2400, but seas not yet high enough to cause reducing standard convoy speed of 10 knots.

All had dramatically changed by dawn on the 8th. In the wheelhouse the revolution indicator read 85 turns, convoy forward progress down to six knots, zigzagging curtailed to reduce pounding. Of first importance on the bridge was to hang onto anything handy to keep from being tossed about. Green water cascaded over the bow on each plunge into giant seas, water and foam propelled heavenward to cannonade against the superstructure, followed by foaming white water curling over the fantail on the climb up the next charging sea. Shrieking winds of hurricane force churned sea surfaces to swirling foam, clouds of spindrift flew to leeward of heightened wave crests that towered above the frigate's bridge as the ship plummeted downslope from crest to trough. Throughout the morning Altgeld, Taloa and PCE 880 seldom arose into view through storm roiled mist. Shortly into the mid-watch, Altgeld signaled fear of breaking up, the convoy at the time about 200 miles southwest of Kodiak and forty miles east of Chirikof Island. A full load of bulk fuel was taking a toll on Altgeld's integrity. A crack had developed and was progressively lengthening across the width of her main deck immediately abaft the midship superstructure. Over the PA came orders to prepare for severe rolling as the frigate would soon come about on a radical change of course to take up station abeam of the tanker. By blinker, PCE 880 and Taloa were instructed to standby. At speeds just enough to maintain steerage, Altgeld commenced shaping a course to make a lee at Chirikof Island, but then maneuvered to take the seas on her quarter and hove to signaling that the break had worsened and now stretched across the deck from rail to rail. With decks awash, seas mountainous and winds gusting in excess of 70 knots, little could be done in preparation for rescue other than to keep the distressed vessel under close observation in the fading afternoon.

A flashing blinker message from Altgeld at 1630 read, "Captain reports she is cracking more but thinks he can ride it out," followed a few minutes later with, "We have dumped some cargo to relieve stress." In the failing light the struggling tanker was instructed not to darken ship, show all navigation lights, and that Albuquerque would maintain searchlight cover after nightfall. A message at 1800 lessened fears for the tanker, "Have discharged part of cargo fore and aft. Strain partly relieved. Have stopped cracking for a while." At 2035 the tanker was asked, "In your condition do you deem it advisable proceed destination or return to port of departure if wind and sea moderates?" Altgeld quickly replied, "Ship unable to stand rough weather. Captain advises return to port of departure." Near midnight with winds falling off, *Altgeld* set a course for return to Kodiak, speed three knots. At this point PCE 880 was instructed to proceed to destination Dutch Harbor with *Taloa*. As dawn broke on the 9th the frigate readied to take the tanker in tow, but with winds astern and down to Force 3 and her deck break contained by rigged chains, *Altgeld* was able to increase speed and proceed unassisted. Twenty-four hours later the frigate led the tanker into Kodiak. A number of *Altgeld* crewmen visited *Albuquerque* to express gratitude for standing by during the storm. With unconcealed emotion a lone seaman volunteered that *Albuquerque* looked like Jesus Christ walking on water at the height of the storm, prepared to take each seaman by hand had the endangered tanker broken up. No one cared to speculate on the number of survivors had the ship sunk at nightfall on the 8th.

With all six frigates of CortDiv 27 on station by the end of October, convoys working in company with two frigates at the same time became more common. On 14 November *Albuquerque* and *Hoquiam* cleared Dutch Harbor on a mission to rendezvous in Unimak Pass with USS *Orizaba* (AP-24), on scene with replacement troops for various Army posts in the western Aleutians. *Orizaba* was of ancient vintage but capable of 18 knots and with winter closing in, the frigates were in for a rough passage via Adak and Amchitka to arrive in Attu on the 19th. Completing her replacement tasks in Attu and bursting with soldiers eager to be home for Christmas, *Orizaba* signaled departure at 1700 on the 22nd. *Hoquiam* remained in Attu for Guard Ship patrol and *Tacoma* joined up for her baptism of high speed heavy weather steaming on a run for Unimak Pass, 1,200 miles east of Attu. In spite of nasty weather through the night, the two frigates and the old transport held to speeds of 16 knots. Below decks resembled a roller coaster ride, seas rushing by with a swishing sound and pounding action as the frigates crested a wave only to fly downhill headed for a shattering Kaboom!, slamming into a trough, and for moment seemingly coming to a halt before gathering power and with a shudder from stem to stern begin scaling the next sea only to repeat the slide and crash again and again. The cooks abandoned plans for Thanksgiving dinner the next day, Thursday the 23rd, and just as well when heavy seas forced *Albuquerque* to break ranks for emergency repairs to stove in No.1 3-inch gun tub and cracked telephone hookup on the forward main battery. On the 24th, continued pounding forced both escorts to secure sound gear and reduce convoy speed to 13 knots. At 0800 on the 25th, Scotch Cap light in Unimak Pass lay abeam, and once east of the pass *Orizaba* detached to proceed independently. Flashing a foaming wake and soon hull down on the horizon, the old girl gave every intent of a Christmas homecoming for her passengers, leaving her two escorts to come about and at all possible speed shape a course for Dutch Harbor. The flying run with *Orizaba* under winter seas and temperatures hovering near the freezing mark had covered just over 2,200 miles, later said to be the fastest escort run of the war along the chain.

What turned out to be a long and welcome port dalliance in Dutch Harbor for

Albuquerque, 25 November to 14 December, ended abruptly midway through the evening film with the piping of special sea detail and immediate departure on orders from Harbormaster NOB in answer to a distress call from USAT *North Wind,* hard aground and breaking up in heavy seas on an outer island in the Shumagins off Cold Bay, a point about 200 miles east of Unimak Pass and at least fourteen hours steaming time from Dutch Harbor. *Albuquerque* slipped her moorings at ABD and nimbly cranked up to all ahead full upon rounding Spithead light. Pouring over the charts, the quartermaster noted the location of the wreck at 54° 53' N and 159" 10' W, a point coinciding with tiny Chernabura Island in the Shumagin group. With the island abeam to port at 1450 the next day, USAT *David Branch* was identified maneuvering in sight of the wreck. It was soon clear that *North Wind* was beyond salvage and rapidly breaking up, her main deck awash and seas breaking over her superstructure decks. *Branch* advised that two boats had cleared the wreck before her arrival and that her motor lifeboat was now alongside to rescue the remaining crew. In the face of an icy wind, the frigate stood in toward the wreck to form a lee for the lifeboat. The boat departed the wreck but lost headway in breaking waves and then lost the first line fired by Lyle gun from the frigate. Precious minutes lost, a second line was fired and this time held fast. The four inch line followed and at a shout from the bowhook answered by the cry of "haul away," the boat in no time scraped alongside *Albuquerque's* lee fantail, and none too soon. From an all but swamped boat, eighteen *North Wind* survivors, including the Chief Officer, Chief Engineer, a Navy ensign and an Army chaplain scrambled aboard, followed by *Branch's* Chief Officer and four boat crew. All *North Wind* hands were accounted for when a radio message from Liberty ship *Carl Schurz* reported that remaining crew from two lifeboats were safely aboard. *Schurz* joined up and in line of three, the frigate zigzagging in the lead, the convoy made for Dutch Harbor, arriving unannounced at 0315 Sunday, 17 December. The Seattle Post Intelligencer, January 5, 1945, carried a front page story beginning with:

> "Dramatic details of a hazardous North Pacific rescue of 55 men from the stricken army supply freighter *North Wind* were disclosed by the army and the coast guard here yesterday with arrival in Seattle *of* 18 of the survivors. Participating in the daring mercy operation in pounding, gale-whipped waters off Cold Bay, in the Aleutians, were a coast guard vessel and the army transport *David W. Branch.* Thanks to the joint cooperation of the two services, not a life was lost in the nearly 12 hours it took to save the crew after the ship was swept off course in a storm late on the night of December 14."

Christmas and the new year 1945 were at hand when *Albuquerque* and *Tacoma* cleared Kuluk Bay, Adak, bound for Attu at dusk on the 21st of December escorting old fleet oiler *Brazos* AO-4 and Liberty ship *Carl Schurz.* The usual dirty winter weather developed into a nasty storm by dawn on the 22nd. On the morning watch, *Brazos* steaming 400 yards off *Albuquerque's* starboard quarter surfaced from time to time awash in foam only to disappear in a plunge into the next giant sea. The Liberty ship trailing *Brazos* labored to the crest of wind heightened seas, her stern then lifting skyward to reveal an aimlessly turning propeller whose blades upon digging in on the down slope slapped the water with a pow! pow! pow!, sounding very much like the distant firing of a 40mm gun. Screening to the rear, *Tacoma* seldom arose to view through mist, rain and spindrift. Rain turned to snow late in the day, and after dark conditions were perfect for a surprise burst of Sl. Elmo's Fire, witnessed by *Albuquerque's* bridge watch. The first discharge of white light outlined the mast, spar and radar antenna and a few moments later a second discharge sped around the top of the forward main battery gun tub. St. Elmo's Fire commonly occurs in cold water seas, most frequently in bad weather and in this case just as Longfellow described:

Last night I saw St. Elmo's stars,

With their glittering lanterns all at play,

On the tops of masts and tips of spars,

And I knew we should have foul weather today.

Even dismal, unknown to the Gods, Attu, lost somewhere west of the 180th Meridian, snug in an arbitrary bend in the International Date Line that allows the same calendar day as all of North America, was a welcome "any port in a storm" to the battered frigate sailors. For now it was Christmas Eve. The two frigates moored to either side of West Navy Pier in snow-sodden Massacre Bay, and gratitude not spurned, both crews celebrated Christmas dinner on an even keel. *Albuquerque* made for Adak on the 27th escorting *Schurz* for a quick turn around while *Tacoma* readied to relieve *Pasco* on Guard Ship Station off the Komandorskis. Moored to repair ship *Black Hawk* in Sweeper Cove, Adak, a dead silence unbroken by not a single whistle blast greeted a handful of *Albuquerque* sailors foolish enough to huddle in an icy wind on the leeward side of the stack to welcome in 1945. On the 6th, the frigate departed Adak alone at all possible speed, for return to Attu to arrive on the 7th to moor alongside *Pasco*. *Pasco* had been through a particularly violent bit of bad weather on Guard Ship Station, now pleased to abandon Attu and make for Dutch Harbor and later in the month to slip away to Seattle and duty along the Northwest coast. As it turned out, *Albuquerque* was in for an extended tour of lonely patrols lasting until mid-February in unending beastly weather, relieved twice by *Tacoma* and twice by *Everett*. Once relieved for the second time, *Tacoma,* ailing after four months in the Bering Sea, limped off stateside for extensive overhaul. Shortly before CortDiv 27 reduced in numbers with the departure of *Pasco* and *Tacoma,* Commander Task Force 91 sent a communication to the division via *Tacoma* --050104Z CONFIDENTIAL: CTF 91 SENDS TO COMCORTDIV 27 WHO GIVES BY HAND TO TACOMA X ALSO ACTION SAUSALITO HOQUIAM ALBUQUERQUE EVERETT AND PASCO X ALL HANDS CARRY OUT WITH YOU IN ADDITION TO MEMORIES OF FOG RAIN AND WIND A SINCERE NAVY QUOTE WELL DONE UNQUOTE.

David Hendrickson

Aug. 13, 1995 Tri-City Herald

38a

Violent Bering waters tested mettle of ship's crew

■ Jack Chambers went to war 50 years ago — against the Japanese and against the sea. He was aboard the USS Pasco, returning from patrol between Paramushiro and the Aleutians, when the storm hit. Here is Chambers' account of weather so violent it's lodged in his memory a half-century later.

By JACK CHAMBERS
Special to the Herald

Gale-force winds hit the Pasco, and the crew knew we were in for it.

I was on watch in the radar room next to the bridge. When I saw the captain, executive officer and several other officers on the bridge at the same time, I knew a very serious state of concern had taken over the ship.

The chief quartermaster was at the helm of the Pasco. I had never seen this before, even when we had tied up at Treasure Island. The tide that sweeps in and out of San Francisco Bay creates a very fast current and many a ship has been pushed right by or into the dock.

The storm was gaining and the torrential rains that accompanied the winds were creating tremendous waves. The barometer continued to drop. At times it was difficult to distinguish the ocean from the sheets of water and spray that covered the ship.

"Eye of the storm" was a term I heard many times from the bridge. The ship was very close to capsizing, and the captain had the navigator reading out the degree the ship was rolling.

The Pasco was in a full-blown hurricane now. I was wondering if we were going to survive. It didn't look good. Escaping the storm was out of the question, and now we could only hope there was enough knowledge on the bridge to get us out of this problem.

Ocean waves were breaking over the top of our ship's mast as the ship lay in the trough of the wave. Many times we went

Chambers in WWII   Chambers in 1983

past the point at which we were (expected) to roll over.

The Pasco lay almost flat on its side at times.

About four hours passed under these conditions, and now the winds were letting up a little. The barometer was beginning to rise.

Many ships have been claimed by the rough waters of the Bering Sea, but good seamanship by the captain had saved the Pasco on this wintry day in the Pacific.

It was good to see Attu off the port side of our ship the next day.

Jack Chambers photos

LEFT: The USS Pasco smashes through a wave while on patrol in the Bering Sea. **RIGHT:** Desolate rock, weathered by North Pacific gales, marks Dutch Harbor, Alaska, a port frequented by the USS Pasco while it was on convoy and life-saving duty in World War II

By early 1945, American forces were gearing up for Iwo Jima and Okinawa and the final push to the Japanese homeland. As long as the 11th Air Force continued nuisance raids on the Kurils, raids intended to discourage Japan from moving forces south to the hot war in the western Pacific, the frigates on Guard Ship Station had a role to play. On patrol, however, it all seemed a waste of time. Hour after hour, day after day, on watch in waters totally devoid of anything to report, tired eyes stared off to the horizon on heaving cold gray seas.

Into this vital non-shooting war, checking in one-by-one in January 1945, sentenced to the Aleutians to end their war days before ending up in Russian hands, came the Philippine veterans *Bisbee, Gallup, Rockford, Muskogee, Carson City* and *Burlington*. With patrol, escort duty, dock space and mooring buoys now shared among ten frigates, the Aleutians seemed overrun with frigates, at times found moored three deep in Sweeper Cove, Adak, and alongside Ballyhoo and ABD docks in Dutch Harbor.

Albuquerque's first meeting with the new crowd was upon return to Attu after her last patrol in mid-February. Swinging at a buoy, morning routine was interrupted to moor *Muskogee* from Adak alongside. Her high number 49 seemed to indicate a new ship of greenhorns, believed so since CortDiv 27 numbers were all single digit. A minor confrontation took place when an *Albuquerque* wise guy leaned over the fantail railing to call out, "Hi sailors, how are things in the States?" quickly challenged by "What the hell war did you win?" and "Too bad you weren't with us at Leyte!" Amidst rising exchanges, the *Muskogee* gang wasted no time making it clear that they had departed Leyte in December for Pearl Harbor and then straight to the Bering Sea without so much as a distant view of the California coast. A final low blow was delivered by *Albuquerque* before securing for noon chow, "Okay, so you're heroes of the South Seas, but just wait until you've been through a couple Bering Sea storms. You'll wish to hell you were back sunbathing in Leyte Gulf, which is probably what you did mostly anyway!" This exchange of views occurred on the very day that the Marines stormed ashore on Iwo Jima, 19 February 1945. On the 23rd, the day the Marines raised the flag on Mount Suribachi, the two frigates were buttoned down in heavy weather shepherding Liberty ship *Christopher Greenup* bound for Adak at a wallowing eight knots, a speed which added an extra day to the continuing boredom of Bering Sea escort.

By April it was clear that the war was drawing down in the Aleutians. Welcome port time was more the order of the day with fewer ships to escort as the need for war materials and supplies declined and reduction in forces along the chain progressed. Further evidence that wartime conditions were winding down occurred with the return of the Aleuts who had been evacuated to southeastern Alaska in 1942. *Albuquerque* escorted the first returning Aleuts into Nazan Bay, Atka Island, on 27 April. Then on to Adak on 1 May to find Sweeper Cove bulging with ships crowding docks and mooring buoys and just enough space to moor outboard of *Rockford* and *Burlington* at Pier 9. The Paramushiro raiders, cruisers *Raleigh* and

Richmond, rode at anchor in Kuluk Bay. Grumbling and grousing over the boring repetition of it all, the 20mm gun crews of the three frigates were bussed off to Andrew Lagoon to expend uncounted magazines of ammo. The joke passed around that brushing up on skills was second to getting rid of surplus fire power. With no end in sight of the Pacific war as far as frigate sailors could see, the end of the war in Europe on the 8th of May, aroused little cheer other than the offer to fire away at Andrew Lagoon in celebration.

Toil worn *Albuquerque* slipped out of Adak under cover of darkness on the 18th as single ship escort for freighter *Taloa* on a nine day tour, first to Amchika, then on to Attu, back to Adak and finally to destination Dutch Harbor, arriving on Sunday, 27 May. Moored three deep to Ballyhoo Dock, scuttlebutt swirled like wild fire on frigates *Albuquerque, Hoquiam* and *Bisbee,* all versions of departure for the States. Sunday the 3rd of June dawned under a rare cloudless sky, so unknown that the slopes of Mt. Ballyhoo were soon alive with wandering sailors. Not to last, Tuesday, 5 June 1945, rose in the usual grip of low gray overcast concealing all terrain above a couple hundred feet in elevation, but to the mess deck crowd at noon chow aboard *Albuquerque* the day turned bright and cheerful beyond belief. The voice of the captain on the PA calmly announced that CortDiv 27 was bound for Seattle and that *Albuquerque* would set special sea detail at 1300. To cries of disbelief, someone pointed out the irony of exactly fourteen months to the day since dropping lines at Pier 41, Seattle. At all ahead full in fair weather, Cape Flattery light rose to starboard at 0100 on the 10th, four and a half days out of Dutch Harbor. At dusk on the previous day with *Albuquerque* in the lead, *Sausalito, Hoquiam* and *Everett* joined up and in line of four, homecoming pennants flying from the peaks of masts, the frigates stood into Strait of Juan de Fuca and on to Puget Sound and the naval shipyard at Bremerton for assignment to various yards for refit in preparation for transfer to the USSR. One month later all six frigates of CortDiv 43 departed the Aleutians on a similar passage to Seattle waters. No longer identified as Escort Divisions 27 and 43, now under orders of Commander Alaska Sea Frontier, twelve frigates ended their Coast Guard-manned careers in August 1945 in Cold Bay, Alaska, when the colors were hauled down and the ships formally transferred to the Soviet Union.

Albuquerque (PF-7) leaving Dutch Harbor, Aleutian Islands, for Seattle, 5 June 1945.

For ne'er can sailor salty be
Until he sails the Bering Sea,
And views Alaska's dreary shore
And fills himself with Arctic lore.

Columbus and Balboa too,
With Nelson form a salty crew,
But they are fresh to you and me —
They never sailed the Bering Sea.

So when you boast of fiercest gale,
That ever ocean you did sail,
You can not salty sailor be
Until you cruise the Bering Sea.

  — Trident Society *The Book
    of Navy Songs.*[2]

Priest Rock, entering Dutch Harbor

Dutch Harbor, Alaska
53°55' N. Latitude -- 166°30' W. Longitude

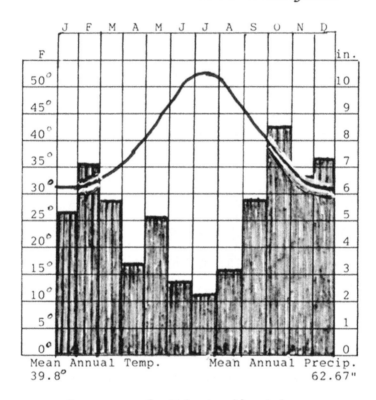

Mean Annual Temp. 39.8°

Mean Annual Precip. 62.67"

Seasonal Distribution
of
Rainfall and Temperature

Divine site. The Russian Orthodox Church of the Holy Ascension is one of the oldest churches in Alaska.

40c

Officer complement, USS Albuquerque (PF-7), upon return to Seattle, June 1945
CO: Lt. R.C. Sweet and XO: Lt. L.C. Powell : to left and right of stub mast

40d

USS ALBUQUERQUE PF-7

2nd Division dockside at Attu 1944

David Hendrickson

In dedication to the patrol frigate crews of the Aleutians and the Bering Sea
Whose ships went to the USSR under Lend-Lease at Cold Bay

Albuquerque, Bisbee, Burlington, Carson City, Everett, Gallup
Hoquiam, Muskogee, Pasco, Rockford, Sausalito, Tacoma

We salute you, Bering Sea!
Your waves of tossing brine,
Your hills of rolling white caps,
Your glacial acres shine.

From Attu's shore..both up and down,
Wherever fierce winds blow
Your face is carved by ice and sleet
And clouds of driving snow

Tossing and churning, you cavort about
Playing with the fate of man,
Freezing your furrowed brow
With the great storm's icy hand

We respect you, Bering Sea,
For your cold, your rage and might,
For when we sailed your towering crests
You showed us how to fight!

Written and submitted by Russell Powell, USS Carson City PF-50

CHAPTER 4

Tales of the North Atlantic

Of the forty-five frigates built in the six Great Lakes yards, all but the four that joined the Seventh Fleet in the Southwest Pacific served in the Atlantic and adjacent waters. Following launching and under their own power they made it to Chicago, nearly 1,000 miles from Superior, Wisconsin, at the far western end of lake Superior and a like distance from as far east as Cleveland, Ohio, on Lake Erie. Upon converging at Chicago, all faced the lengthy ferry procedure down the inland waterway, raised by pontoons to a draft of no more than nine feet and somewhere along the Illinois River below Chicago lashed as just another barge to a barge and tow operation for the week's journey down the Mississippi to the Gulf of Mexico. (See Captain Earle's account of the *Greensboro,* Great Lakes to the Gulf). Outfitting in preparation for commissioning and shakedown off Bermuda took place in Louisiana and Texas yards and, for one or more frigates at Charleston and Curtis Bay, near Baltimore. The greatest number, nineteen, were converted for weather patrol during post-shakedown availability. Weather ships were immediately identified by the box affair or "hanger" for inflating weather balloons that replaced the after 3-inch gun. The second greatest number, sixteen, were visible from late 1944 to the end of the European war in May 1945, guiding convoys from Norfolk to Oran, Algeria, in the Mediterranean. *Key West, Brunswick, Gulfport* and *Uniontown* shared honors for the most trips -three round trips each. Oran was a major marshaling port for goods destined for Allied troops surging across the Rhine in Germany and those wiping up Italy. *Newport, Gloucester, Poughkeepsie, Evansville* and *Bath* were detained in service on the Eastern Sea Frontier for coastal escort, patrol and training duties until sent to Seattle for refit and Lend-Lease, becoming the last ships transferred to the Soviets before the program ended on 5 September 1945.

If there ever was a duty that tried a sailor's soul and stamina, it must have been weather patrol in the North Atlantic. Working out of frigid and barren Argentia, Newfoundland, day upon day, week upon week, month after month, often returning to Argentia sheathed in ice to the point of instability, and only brief periods of availability to look forward to in Boston or Bermuda for storm inflicted repairs, was a form of sea duty that no sailor in the Pacific would have traded for. Not that Argentia was completely without its attractions as watertender John Buscemi of *Woonsocket* put it:

> Our home port was Argentia We used to go to the Navy PX where we would see Newfoundland girls working. Due to lack of calcium they were missing some of their front teeth which made them unattractive. However, after returning from patrol they started looking better, until after the fourth patrol they looked beautiful. After returning from repairs in Boston they

again looked unattractive. And then we went to Bermuda for repairs where all sailors had to be back aboard ship by 5 pm and signs read "Dogs and Sailors keep off the grass."

A total of forty-five patrol frigates built on the Great Lakes made the transit down the inland waterway to New Orleans. The following is a transit account from Cleveland to the Gulf and on to Curtis Bay, Maryland, of the Greensboro (PF-101) by Captain W.K. Earle, USCG (Ret).

In the fall of 1944, I was assigned CO of the *Hingham* (PF-30), then undergoing precommissioning outfitting in New Orleans. Since our commissioning was some months away, Commander W.C. "Wild Bill" Hogan, CO of Coast Guard personnel in the area and responsible for moving new construction frigates from the Great Lakes to outfitting yards, assigned me to head up a ferrying crew to pick up *Greensboro* at the American Shipbuilding Yard in Cleveland and bring her down the Mississippi to New Orleans. I had done this once before with the *Davenport,* then outfitting at Houston.

New frigates were not accepted by the Navy until delivered to the outfitting yards, so the ships remained the responsibility of the shipbuilding yard during the transit. Shipyard crews sailed the ships to Chicago, then through the Chicago Drainage Canal to Lockport, Illinois, on the Illinois River, where they were pumped out and fitted with tanks to lift them to 8 foot draft. They were then incorporated into large river barge make-ups and transported down river as dead ships by Mississippi River towboats. Ferrying crews of Coastguardsmen, usually people scheduled to man the ship when commissioned, went along to learn the ship and look out for government interests.

My ferrying crew of about 24 officers and men boarded the *Greensboro* in Cleveland and sailed with the shipyard crew. My people stood watches with the civilians and worked to learn the ship's systems. It was good that we learned well. Upon arrival in Chicago, the civilian crew left en masse over some labor dispute. The ship had to be in Lockport the next day if it was to start its scheduled down river transit on time. Delay would have set the program back several weeks and ships were needed for the rapidly expanding North Atlantic Weather Patrol. My mustang chief engineer, a newly commissioned warrant officer, said he could run the engines if I could conn the ship. He assembled an abbreviated black gang. I assembled an abbreviated bridge, conning and line handling detail, only to discover when ready to cast off that my quartermaster, fresh out of school, had not been to sea, had never steered a ship, nor had anyone else in our group ever qualified as a helmsman, save myself, and I had done it only on cadet practice cruises many years earlier.

I remember the tortuous transit of 24 bridges in the Chicago Drainage Canal vividly. A civilian pilot conned from the flying bridge. I steered in response to his voice tube orders, the quartermaster handled the engine order telegraph, and the few hands on deck handled lines and fenders. Somehow we managed to wheel the 304 foot ship through the heart of Chicago without mishap and made it to Lockport in time for the transit down river.

The trip down river was a ball. The towboat that handled the 26 tightly lashed barges that we were attached to did all the work. Though we were a dead ship pumped high and dry, we used emergency generators for electrical power, had sufficient potable water, and were blessed with a great cook who managed to scrounge up truly gourmet chow. With minimal watches to stand and no navigational responsibilities, we spent much time lounging in the sun in deck chairs, dining prodigiously, reading, listening to radio music, and watching the lovely countryside of the American heartland slip by. At night we'd be tied up to pilings, occasionally to stout trees along the riverbank. It was Mark Twain river boating at its best.

Once in New Orleans, signals changed. *Greensboro* was to go to Curtis Bay for outfitting. We had to work fast, the crew beefed up to 70 men, radio gear and guns hastily installed, the ship placed "in service" (status as a U.S. vessel), and in less than a week we took off on *Greensboro's* first sea voyage. Though most of the crew had not been to sea and my experience only two years as a junior officer on *Campbell,* we got that ship to Curtis Bay without mishap. Seasickness was our greatest enemy. We weathered a storm off Hatteras, made a landfall off Cape Henry and a night time transit up Chesapeake Bay, and even managed a smart landing at Curtis Bay on a bright morning, by God!

116

The Globe Shipbuilding Corp.-built USS Covington (PF-56) as modified during 30 Nov. 1944 through 20 Dec. 1944 for weather ship duty. Note the hangar aft for weather balloons. Official USN Photograph, Boston NY No. 7207-44 taken 20 Dec. 1944. Covington was underway from 0820 through 1430 on the 20th, running the degaussing range, calibrating compasses and the DAQ direction finder. The ship departed Boston the 22nd for Argentia, Newfoundland, weather duty.

Another Great Lakes (Leathem D. Smith)-built ship, USS Davenport (PF-69), seen at Charleston Navy Yard on 26 June 1945. Official USN Photograph, Charleston No. 1761-45, (other views in this series are NH 82145/6). Davenport was modified for weather ship duty at Charleston NY from 10 to 25 June 1945, spending 15 to 19 June in Dry Dock #2 as well. The ship departed Charleston for Argentia at 0709 on 26 June.

USS Woonsocket (PF-32)

41d
The boys from the Woonsocket on escape from Argentia living it up in Bermuda

41e

USS Evansville (PF-70) en route to Bermuda for shakedown, December 1944

On the other hand, Frank Intagliata of the *Groton* remembers Argentia as the place where President Roosevelt and Winston Churchill signed the agreement that turned fifty destroyers over to the British before the United States entered the war, and the place where the *Groton* crew spent time between patrols in log cabins at Recreation Camp. As Frank put it: "After 30 days on patrol, the camp was a welcome place." In his remembrance note, Frank recalls the weather and location of patrols:

> The weather in the North Atlantic. It is hard to put in words the feeling that one experiences. The *Groton's* hull was made of 3/8" steel plates. The seams were welded together to form a ship that in rough weather is tossed and twisted at ungodly angles. Many times while on watch in the gyro room, I could hear and feel the continual banging of each wave as we would ride the bottom of a swell to the top of the next one where it would beat against the bow. We all would pray that the welds would hold, and they did. Along with rough seas we encountered an ice field one night. Luckily the sea calmed and we only had to put up with the noise of the ice as the ship maneuvered through the ice. It was a beautiful sight by day. Our patrols were all over the Atlantic, from Greenland south to the Azores, over to Bermuda, then up to straits that led to the North Pole. On northern patrol we encountered icebergs and frequently used them for gunnery practice. One night in the middle of the Atlantic, GQ sounded. Much to our surprise we were surrounded by an antisubmarine unit and were challenged with signals and search lights. Somehow someone failed to use the correct code for the time and day.

Back in Argentia following a lengthy patrol amidst ice fields and icebergs, gunner's mate Tom Bacon of *Groton* went over the side to inspect the hull:

> I had attended the Naval Shallow Water (50') Diving School in Norfolk. As a result, I made a dive on PF-29 to examine the port side damage after hitting or scraping an iceberg in the North Atlantic. My observation was a 4" to 6" gash about 15' to 20' long. I recall breaking water from the dive, holding my hands apart, then stretching my arms as wide as I could to show the vertical crack.

North Atlantic weather duty had a debilitating psychological quality to it (perhaps more so aboard *Emporia* than others--six COs from October 1944 to July 1946), that being

115

the knowledge that you were not going anywhere on patrol but around in circles and back to where you came from, exactly the opposite of the best sea duty of all aboard the large transports like the *Wakefield* or the 600 ft. Admiral and General class APs whose logs noted the likes of New York, Southampton, Marseilles, Naples, Port Said, Capetown, Sydney, New Caledonia, Manila, Pearl Harbor, San Francisco, Los Angeles, Panama Canal, amounting to 50,000 miles or more a year. Frigates that logged uncounted patrols out of Argentia from late 1994 to spring 1946 were *Muskegon, Emporia, Shreveport, Forsyth, Groton, Hingham, Grand Rapids, Woonsocket, Dearborn, Covington, Sheboygan, Abilene, Beaufort, Charlotte, Manitowoc, Lorain, Milledgeville.* Others also known to Argentia are mentioned in connection with alternate duties.

The threat of man overboard was a constant fear aboard weather ships in heavy weather, a sad occurrence experienced by *Emporia* off Greenland on Christmas Eve 1944, as told here by former SM1/c Eugene O'Brien:

David Hendrickson

USS Emporia (PF-28)
Christmas Eve, December 24, 1944
By Eugene P. O'Brien SM1/c USCG

The ship is under command of executive officer Lt. Robert Althauser. Commanding officer Lt. Cmdr. Langford Anderson remained ashore in Boston because of illness. Weather, Rescue, Anti-submarine Patrol Station #9 is located two hundred miles east of Cape Farewell, Greenland. The 2000 to 2400 watch is on war cruising status.

The North Atlantic is in one of its typical December moods. The sea swells are mountainous, the ship more under the sea than on it, the wind a constant howl, the superstructure coated with ice. From time to time St Elmo's Fire runs along the mast and rigging. The crew has just finished an hour of breaking ice from the starboard side. The gigantic swells have no set direction. The engines are making turns for ten knots just keeping the bow into the sea. After five days the weather broke and a sighting was taken. The ship was twelve miles further back than thought to be.

Thank God for the Great Lake ship builders, the hull remained sound, not one weld had split open. The splinter shield around No. 1 three inch gun was laid flat. The ready ammunition box holding twenty-four hedgehog rockets was torn loose and driven aft to lodge against the bridge stanchions. Secured by life lines, two hands lifted each rocket from the racks and heaved them overboard.

Life lines are rigged from bridge ladders to the weather shack. All hands on watch hang on for dear life. My station is telephone talker and lookout on the starboard 40mm amidships. Each time the bow breaks the surface, the ship leaps into the air and comes down with a resounding roar. PF-28 shudders from stem to stern. The Red Badge of Courage for North Atlantic PF sailors.

About mid watch Lt. Robert Thayer, assistant first lieutenant, appeared at my station and instructed me to accompoany him to the bridge. We were relieving the helmsman and bridge talker every hour. I turned the phones over to shipmate Ray Knowles FC 3/c. My last words to him were,"Ray, don't leave the mount, keep a tight lifeline, the seas are breaking over the main deck here."
Lt. Thayer and I waited for an opportunity and on his signal made a mad dash along the life line to the bridge ladder, up the side of the wardroom to the next level where was located the wheel house, captain's sea cabin and chart/radar room. As we reached the top of the ladder, a gigantic swell engulfed the ship from stack to fantail. Lt. Thayer remarked, "Thank God we made it, another minute and you and I would be gone forever."

I relieved the helm and together with QM1/c Charles Pearstein tried to keep the ship pointed in the right direction, me on the wheel and Pearstein on the engine order telegraph. Just then I heard the bridge talker tell the OD, Ens. John Roberts, ship's communication officer, that he could not raise the starboard 40mm lookout for the periodic check. My heart skipped a beat. That was my shipmate and friend Ray Knowles they were talking about. Boatswain's mate of the watch Bellezo went to investigate and minutes later returned to the bridge to report that lookout Ray Knowles was gone. He had been swept over the side by that huge sea. The evidence was two broken cable rails and snapped telephone cable.

There was no thought of coming about in the heavy seas following the "man overboard" call. The risk of loss of the ship was too great, safety of the ship and crew paramount. The fantail was searched to no avail. Days later the ship returned to the area to find nothing. God spared the ship and crew and in true USCG fashion the mission was completed. The ship suffered extensive damage on the weather decks during the long storm.

There was many a teary eye on the mess deck that night. Ray Knowles was our first casualty and he gave his life for his country the same as those lost under fire.

42b

On Christmas Day Lt.Thayer emptied Ray's locker and packed his sea bag for shipment home to his family. MM2/c Bill Heyden and I assisted in packing the sea bag. Ray and Bill often played crib together. Bill's peg board was in Ray's locker. He didn't have the courage to ask for it when it appeared.

Every Christmas at Midnight Mass I remember the incident and Ray Knowles' smiling face. As I reflect, "There but for the grace of God went I," and I think of the sad Christmas message received by the Knowles family - Ray's mother, father and sister.

U.S.COAST GUARD official dispatch - unit ACADEMY - 23 December 1944, heading 231647
TEXT

FOR SENIOR CHAPLAIN. REFER CIRCULAR 211 NOTIFY CLARENCE KNOWLES 255 ELLSWORTH AVENUE NEW HAVEN CONN THAT HIS SON RAYMOND DANIEL KNOWLES FIRECONTROLMAN THIRD USCGR WASHED OVERBOARD FROM VESSEL BY HEAVY SEA TWENTY TWO DEC. WHEN ADDITIONAL INFORMATION AVAILABLE WILL ADVISE DIRECT. EXPRESS SINCERE REGRETS OF NAVY DEPARTMENT AND COMMANDANT COAST GUARD. ADVISE THIS OFFICE WHEN NOTIFICATION ACCOMPLISHED.

COPIES TO: FILE
          COMMUNICATIONS
          CHAPLAIN HODGKINS
          PERSONNEL

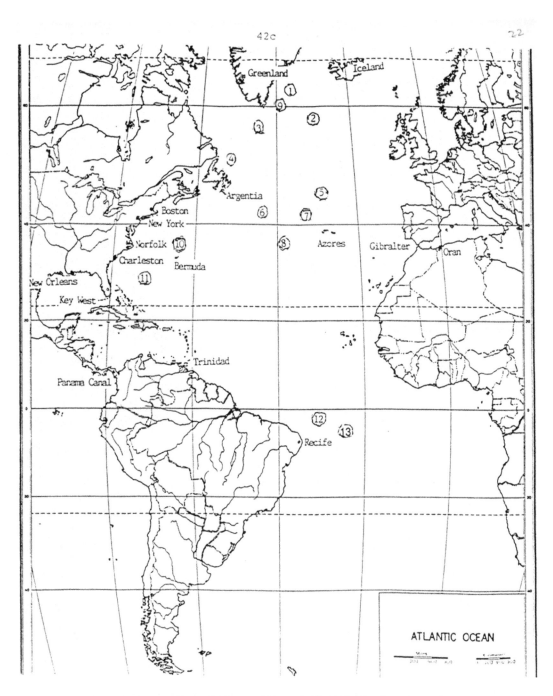

Weather Stations 1 -- 13 patrolled by patrol frigates in World War II and post-war until early 1946. From time to time station numbers and locations changed from "old" to "new."

Groton (PF-29) crunching through an ice field at dawn off Greenland, winter 1944

Groton (PF-29) taking the measure of an iceberg off Greenland, winter 1944.

Groton (PF-29) *takes on a load of unwanted ice off Greenland, winter 1944.*

Your normal every day sea in the North Atlantic aboard Groton (PF-29)

42h

USS *Greensboro* (PF-101)

USS *Racine* (PF-100)

Storm damage took its toll on the weather ships to the extent that availability for repairs kept the yards in Boston, Bermuda and Argentia supplied with a steady stream of customers. In one case, damage was so severe that, following inspection, *Davenport* was ordered to report to Commandant, First Naval District for disposition. The severe damage occurred on an October 1945 patrol, and with the war over, a lengthy estimated repair time no doubt contributed to the decommissioning decision. *Davenport* had an early career of escort duty to Oran before conversion to weather duty.

Topside storm damage most commonly amounted to caved in gun tubs, loosened ready boxes, broken telephone hookups at gun mounts, twisted depth charge racks and occasional loss of depth charges, and at times swept away life rafts. Below the waterline damage was largely limited to failure of bilge keel welds and sea pounding damage to the sonar dome. (Ed. note: Bilge keels to reduce rolling were fins attached to the ship's bottom where the vertical turns to become the horizontal described as the turn of the bilge. On the frigates a bilge keel section was 20'4" long, 1'4" wide and 2" thick. A weld failure at the forward end of the bilge keel would work aft, the keel folding back and chaffing against the hull, or in some cases wrenching loose and dropping away). Machinist mate Bill Deyoe of *Manitowoc* told in a letter,"... On one patrol we lost all bilge keels on the port side, and half of them on the starboard side, which caused a leak in the engine room. We had our relief ship escort us into Argentia for repairs in dry dock." But storm damage aside, Bill recalled that life aboard *Manitowoc* "... was like being on a cruise ship. We had the oldest movies of all, but we also had gambling in different places on the ship, and midnight snacks, but only if you were in the Black Gang. We even went swimming when we were on a southern patrol."

On patrol on Station 2 at 58 degrees N -37 degrees W in November 1944, *Muskegon* took a pounding for fifteen days with winds at times recorded at 80 knots. The frigate was swept by a massive *wave* on the 1st of December causing extensive damage subject to repair in Argentia. On 24 April 1945, *Muskegan* was called off station to assist destroyer *Eberle* in search of a U-boat near Monhegan Island in the Gulf of Maine, an action which had the frigate steaming 200 yards offshore at flank speed in eighteen feet of water making for Roaring Bull Rock Buoy where surface smoke was thought to be diesel emission from the U-boat snorkel. Depth charge and hedgehog attack resulted in no contact. Back in Boston, *Muskegon* was assigned the role of ammunition ship loaded with 1,000 hedgehogs lashed on deck and crammed into passageways and available compartments for transportation to Argentia. Like many of her sisters, *Muskegon* continued on weather patrol after the war, her role expanded to assist air navigation. To make her more visible to an aircraft in trouble, her once gray decks and bridge were repainted a brilliant yellow as a form of, as one observer put it, reverse camouflage that did little to improve her appearance as a ship of war. *Knoxville* and others were awarded the same color scheme.

On Weather Station 5 out of Argentia, *Forsyth* on 12 May 1945 received a radio report that a U-boat in her area somewhere was seeking to surrender. In dicey weather and fog the search was on. *Forsyth* came upon the surfaced U-234 to join up with Navy DE *Sutton* standing by to complete the surrender. The submarine, reported on her way to Japan, was carrying high ranking German air force officers, aerial maps of targets in the United States and two Japanese officials, both of whom committed suicide before the surrender. *Sutton* took the German passengers and most of the U-boat crew aboard and with the PF and DE escorting, set course for the U.S. *Forsyth* was requested to send her surgeon aboard the sub to assist the German doctor in an emergency operation on an American sailor, accidentally shot when a Mauser pistol went off in the hands of another American while collecting small arms. Following the operation, the injured sailor was transferred to *Forsyth* for delivery to Argentia, where he later died from internal bleeding.

Charlotte had a brief encounter with a U-boat on a nasty rough seas patrol, her topside locked in more ice than the crew could chip away, guns included. The frigate came upon a surfaced sub in the same iced condition. Joe Brogan reports that the two vessels took the measure of each other, neither able to fire a weapon. "... Finally Captain Dean made contact with the sub skipper. It was a no-win situation--we could ram and sink them but in doing so would put our ship in danger. There was no help within 600 miles. It was agreed that both ships would head south on courses ninety degrees apart so that when ice was cleared the ships would be separated by several hundred miles."

Weather ships were not only endangered by violent seas and ice on the fringes of the Arctic, but were equally endangered by hurricanes on the more southerly stations. Former South Pacific frigate, *Eugene,* spent three days, 24-27 June 1945, of her first weather patrol riding out a hurricane on Station 10. At one point a fire room failure caused loss of power, the frigate then sliding downslope into a deep trough. Years later, her skipper, Lt. Cdr. Henry Hilliard, described what followed: "She was broadside to the huge seas. Then she showed us her qualities. Our *Eugene* rolled, but not dangerously, and lifted up the sides of the waves. I was proud of her. At first I thought we were done for. Great sea-keeping ability." With power restored, *Eugene* completed her patrol.

Lorain, Milledgeville and *Greensboro* were awarded a brief respite from the bitter cold of the North Atlantic by reassignment for operations as a unit of Task Force 26 based in Recife, Brazil, in support of the Army Air Corps and Army Transport Command redeployment in the South Atlantic. The frigates steamed via Trinidad to arrive at Recife in early December 1945 to undertake alternate patrols on Station 12 until the end of the month, followed by a week's R&R in Trinidad on the return to Argentia. *Shreveport* engineered an escape from Argentia to make Recife on 17 December for patrol on Station 13 in the balmy tropics until 8 March 1946.

The Coast Guard-manned patrol frigates earned their stripes as escort vessels in the far reaches of the Southwest Pacific, the Bering Sea and in the hazardous Atlantic in the latter days of the European War. From the 1st of December 1944 to mid-May 1945, sixteen frigates joined the ranks as escorts for large convoys marshaled in Hampton Roads and Norfolk, bound for Oran, Algeria, through the Straits of Gibraltar into the Mediterranean. The sixteen included *Key West, Huron, Gulfport, Bangor, Annapolis, Gladwyne, Moberly, Knoxville, Uniontown, Reading, Peoria, Brunswick, Davenport, New Bedford, Orlando* and *Racine.* After escort duty, most were converted to weather and aircraft assistance ships until summoned for decommissioning in 1946. Upon return from the Southwest Pacific, *El Paso* and *Eugene* joined the Oran escort crowd for one trip in April 1945 before converting to weather ships.

On 1 December 1944, a convoy of more than 100 ships got underway from Norfolk bound for Oran. Among the eight escorts was the frigate Huron on her first convoy assignment. One of her roles was Medical Guard Duty, which consisted of putting a doctor aboard ships in need. On 8 December, while guiding stragglers to correct convoy stations, Huron was rammed on her starboard side by Liberty ship James Fennimore Cooper, and as recalled by QM2/c Steve Irgens, "I was on watch on the bridge, a foggy early morning, the ship nearly dead in the water after having stopped for some reason. I looked aft and saw a Liberty ship bearing down upon us, and the ship slammed into us with a huge crash right into the engine room area... In a short time the stern was about under water. Unbelievably, none of the crew got more than wet feet. .." All electricity failed and the engine room was abandoned due to flooding. *Huron* sent out distress signals, her position 36° 45' N 47° 01' W. DE-171 arrived to take *Huron* in tow. The frigate jettisoned depth charges and smoke screen generators, transferred one officer and forty-nine men to DE-171 by motor whaleboat and fourteen men to DE-168 by raft, all by mid-afternoon. On the 9th, ninety-eight men were transferred to DE-326 along with much meat and perishables. Collision mats were in place on the 10th and additional mats on the 11th after inspection by a party from ARS-21. The collision victim under tow reached Bermuda on the 15th for emergency repairs before being taken under tow by seagoing tug *Choctaw* bound for Charleston Navy Yard. After repairs, *Huron* saw the war out as Flagship, Fleet Sonar School Squadron, Key West, Florida. "As a postscript to this sea story," writes quartermaster Irgens, "Shortly after the war, I saw a newspaper photo and story of a Liberty ship by the name of *James Fennimore Cooper* passing through the locks of the Panama Canal."

On 11 December 1944, *Knoxville* and *Brunswick* departed Hampton Roads for Oran as escorts for convoy UGS-63, arriving safely at destination on the 28th. The return convoy, GUS-63 numbering seventy-nine ships, departed Oran on 2 January. On the 3rd after clearing the Straits of Gibraltar and twenty-two miles southwest of Cape Spartel, Morocco, Liberty ship Henry Miller steaming as lead ship in the fifth column was torpedoed by U-870. Struck in the forward holds, *Miller was* soon down by the head but stable. *Knoxville* and others initiated a search for the submarine that proved unsuccessful. Nearing dusk, the master of the Liberty ship ordered lifeboats #3 and #4 to take twenty-five seamen, twenty-four armed guard, and the security officer off the ship in case of possible bulkhead failure. Only minutes after casting off, all fifty men were safely aboard *Brunswick* and bound for delivery in Gibraltar the next day. A skeleton crew brought the *Miller* into Gibraltar on the 4th. All hands survived the torpedo attack, but the ship, not so lucky, was declared a CTL (constructive total loss).

Bangor sailed on her first convoy for Oran on 23 January 1945. On her second day out she rescued a boatswain's mate who had fallen overboard from her screening companion *Ericson* (DD-440). The return convoy lost one ship to a torpedo attack. The frigate charged in to take part in a coordinated depth charge attack that failed to produce evidence of a U-boat sinking.

From 6 February to 19 May 1945, *New Bedford* completed two trips to Oran. On the return voyage of her first trip, an Oran stowaway was landed at Gibraltar, next the sudden illness of the chief engineer required transfer to a friendly port hospital, and then a week later a crew member suffered acute appendicitis. A breeches buoy was rigged to *Gladwyne* for her surgeon to swing across chilly Atlantic waters to successfully perform an emergency appendectomy. Public Health Service doctors aboard the frigates became accomplished breeches buoy veterans. On a return voyage from Oran on 5 May 1945, *Racine* raced to SS *Lisner*, sending her surgeon aboard by high line transfer for emergency service. Upon return to *Racine* the Good Samaritan in the breeches buoy was dunked into a foaming swell as the lines slackened between the ships.

Between her two trips to Oran, *Moberly* participated in the last U-boat destruction of the war, 6 May 1945, two days before European hostilities ended. On 2 May, coastal collier *Black Point* sailed from Newport News, Virginia, for Weymouth, Massachusetts. In fog, about five miles southeast of Point Judith, Rhode Island, she was struck by a torpedo at 1740 on 5 May, fired by *U-853*. The collier, badly damaged, capsized and sank twenty-five minutes after the attack, the sinking claiming one Navy armed guard and eleven merchant crewmen. Two foreign freighters picked up survivors. *Moberly* and *Atherton* (DE-169) arrived on scene three hours after the sinking and began a sweep to seaward of Block Island, where the submarine was detected hiding on the bottom in eighteen fathoms of water. *Atherton* made first contact at about 2030 and attacked with both hedgehog and depth charges, followed by *Moberly.* Depth charge attacks continued the next day until destruction of the badly damaged enemy was assured. Large amounts of debris, including an officer's cap had surfaced. *Atherton* was credited with the sinking with *Moberly* assisting. A German submarine silhouette was painted on *Moberly's* bridge, and the crew authorized to wear the Engagement Star in their American Theater ribbon.

David Hendrickson

46a

Foster's Daily Democrat, Dover, N.H.
Monday Evening, May 8, 1995

V-E Day 50th Anniversary

U-boat sunk two-days before V-E Day

Barrington man's ship helps sink sub off R.I.

By EMILY TORGAN
Democrat Staff Writer

BARRINGTON - Milton R. Woodruff sat back and gazed at Ayers Lake from one of his living room armchairs on a brilliant April afternoon.

"I like the lake, but I love the ocean," mused Woodruff, a World War II veteran who readied himself to recount his incredible war memories.

Between 1943 and 1945, Woodruff served as senior sonarman aboard the USS Moberly, the ship which destroyed the last German U-boat sunk in World War II on May 6, 1945, two days before V-E Day.

Woodruff joked that he never intended to take part in the historical event.

"At 19, I chose the Coast Guard because I thought I'd be guarding Boston Harbor," he said.

Instead, Woodruff guarded huge convoys of Allied fleets in almost every theater of naval war, from the American area campaign to the Pacific and North Africa.

The waters were rife with German U-boats, or "sea wolves" which traveled in packs, all hungry to sink the Allied navy.

Woodruff said that then, he was less frightened of the Nazi submarines than the oceans.

"You could fight back the German U-boat, but you couldn't fight the sea," said Woodruff, who was on board for five hurricanes.

He remains nostalgic for the USS Moberly.

"I think about the ship itself," he said. "It was all there was between us and the bottom of the ocean, and it brought us home every time."

Woodruff remembered the ship as "clean living" because the ship did not engage in combat with planes or surface ships.

50th Anniversary

VICTORY **IN** **E**UROPE **DAY**

May 8, 1945 — 1995

"The only danger was the sea wolves," remembered Woodruff, who shook his head.

Woodruff spoke of the tense, constant questions from his fellow seamen. As senior sonarman, Woodruff was responsible for sending out the radio signals that would bounce off solid objects, thus detecting German submarines.

"The men in the engine room asked the most questions," said Woodruff. "If we got torpedoed, they'd never be able to get out."

But finally, after being out to sea for 81 days, May 1945 arrived. The USS Moberly escorted a convoy to New York City, then headed for Boston.

"We were headed for Boston and liberty," recalled Woodruff. "No one could wait to get there."

But a mere 15 miles off the coast of Block Island, R.I., an SOS call shook the radio shack. An American freighter had just been torpedoed off the coast of Block Island. As senior sonarman, Woodruff jumped for his gear.

"We contacted the German captain through morse code, told him the war was over, and asked him to surrender," said Woodruff. But the captain refused.

Soon, the USS Moberly dropped 13 ashcans (full of explosives) onto the submarine.

"That did it," said Woodruff. "A whole bunch of stuff floated to the top, including the captain's hat."

Woodruff said seeing the hat was not an especially satisfying experience.

"We had to do it," Woodruff said. "He'd already sunk one boat, and he would have torpedoed us if he could have. It was them or you."

Woodruff believes World War II was necessary and was proud to go. However, he remembered a day on his ship that involved no violence as his happiest day at sea.

"The U-boat clung to the ocean bottom, and it was in very shallow water," explained Woodruff, who said that made his work particularly problematic because echoes were coming back to him from both the boat and the ocean floor.

But luckily, the USS Moberly had a German sonarman on board who possessed a fine ear for music, who was able to distinguish which echoes were coming from where by listening to the pitches of the echoes.

"It was a beautiful May morning, and we had to go through the Cape Cod canal," said Woodruff, who arrived to find the canal mobbed with cheering civilians.

"They were blowing their horns, clapping and cheering," said Woodruff. "That day, you would have thought we had won the war single-handedly."

129

46b

From account of *Knoxville* (PF-64) -- CO G.R. Reynolds, Capt. USCG (Ret)

High Line Transfer .... In December 1944, *Knoxville* was one of the escorts of a convoy to the Mediterranean. The convoy departed Hampton Roads and made up off the Virginia Capes, joined up by a convoy from New York. The combined convoy had over one hundred ships with an escort of twelve ships, including eleven PFs and DEs and one DD carrying the escort commander.

At the conference before departure, the escort commander looked at the PF skippers and said, "You PFs have a doctor aboard, don't you? I expect you to be ready to transfer him by high line to any ship in the convoy that needs medical assistance." "Yes sir." we responded nervously. We had heard of high line transfer, but high line transfer was not included in our shakedown training nor in any other of our training. We did not have the gear for the job.. Immediately after the conference we called the District Coast Guard office and arranged to pick up an old lifeboat station breeches bouy outfit, minus the Lyle gun and cart.

Sure enough, several days into the convoy we were ordered to put our doctor aboard one of the merchant ships. We used our breeches bouy gear and it worked just fine. Since we had not been drilled in this operation and had been provided no gear, we were free to experiment. We later obtained a seat from a wrecked helicopter and converted it to a much better seat for the doctor to ride in.

We had three doctors while *Knoxville* was in service. Dr. Leon Prince of Philadelphia was our first. He was indeed a prince, and approached the transfer business with complete confidence that we who were conducting the transfer did not necessarily share. He made several transfers in mid Atlantic and then unfortunately for *Knoxville*, we lost him to a shore transfer when his young daughter became gravely ill. When his relief came aboard he confided in me, "I don't know whether I'm qualified for this assignment. When I got married, my wife and I went to Bermuda on our honeymoon. I was seasick every mile of the cruise down and back." As soon as we put to sea, the good doctor took to his bunk and failed even to make daily sick call.

A few days out we were directed by the escort commander to put our doctor aboard a merchant vessel. I immediately sent for the doctor, who after a long delay reached the bridge looking dreadful. I told him he was to be transferred by high line to a ship in the convoy and at that he slowly collapsed on the deck. I then called the escort commander on the TBS explaining the situation and concluding that if he insisted we would make the transfer but in my opinion the doctor would be of no use to the patient. The escort commander cancelled the order to *Knoxville* and gave the assignment to another PF, much to our embarrassment. Upon return to port immediate action was taken to acquire a new doctor.

And that is how we got Dr. Eugene Brodsky. He joined us shortly before we were parmanently assigned to weather patrol. He was very young and adventurous and a great addition to the wardroom. Convoys were discontinued but high line transfers were made to independants carrying troops back to the States. The North Atlantic is seldom calm and Dr Brodsky's transfers were all made under marginal weather conditions. Like Dr. Prince, he approached each transfer with complete confidence.

46c

Racine (PF-100) the wardroom gang, CO Cmdr. Clarence H. Waring fourth from left, commissioning day, Houston, Texas, 22 January 1945.

46d

Racine (PF-100) the CPOs gather for commissioning photo, Houston, Texas, 22 January 1945.

46e

Racine (PF-100) the crew crowds the after forecastle deck for commissioning day photo. Houston, Texas, 22 January 1945.

CHAPTER 5

Farewell to the Patrol Frigates

As the war was winding down in the summer of 1945, every frigate remaining in commission was either an already established weather ship or soon to become one. With increasing transoceanic air traffic, weather ships were called upon to expand service as plane guard and air communication vessels. The qualities of sea kindliness, the high freeboard of the lengthy forecastle deck and the fact that foot traffic moved unhindered on one level from fantail to prow (the full length of the ship) mostly undercover on the main deck, was a great advantage over the DEs, making the frigates acceptable for long and boring spells on lonely mid-ocean stations. Nineteen frigates were transferred from the Navy to the Coast Guard in the final stages of weather service for the frigates, and in any case weather ships continued as Coast Guard responsibility beyond the frigate era, which ended in September 1946. In the period from war's end in 1945 to mid-1946, frigates operated on all stations in the Atlantic and in the Pacific from the Marshalls in eastern Micronesia to the Philippines and Guam in the western Pacific and north to the Bering Sea. So even though most of the original frigates of the North and South Pacific had gone off to join the Russian fleet, some of their sisters returned to the vastness of the Pacific, steaming in pairs serving in relief for each other on assigned stations.

Gulfport and *Orlando* were converted to weather ships in July 1945 at Staten Island, New York, and subsequently sailed in tandem to Pearl Harbor, arriving 5 September for a five day respite before shaping a course for Adak in the Aleutians. From here, they patrolled on weather and plane guard duty on Station "J" 43°N -165°E until May 1946. The two frigates departed Adak for Seattle on 6 May and decommissioning, *Gulfport* on 28 May and *Orlando* on 27 June. Both went to the breakers in November 1947, sold to Zidell Ship Dismantling Co. of Seattle.

Gladwyne and *Moberly* joined up at Boston in July 1945 for conversion to weather ships in preparation for steaming to Pearl Harbor, arriving on 23 August for a few days liberty before making for Majuro in the Marshall Islands of eastern Micronesia. The two sisters patrolled out of Majuro and Kwajalein Atoll until return to Pearl Harbor in mid-December for duty in Hawaiian waters. *Gladwyne* departed Pearl Harbor 2 April 1946 for San Francisco where she was transferred from the Navy to the Coast Guard on 15 April, and immediately assigned plane guard duty out of San Francisco until ordered to Seattle for decommissioning on 31 August. *Gladwyne* was sold to Mexico on 27 November 1947, where she served as the *Papaloapan* until scrapped in 1965. *Moberly* remained in Hawaii patrolling Weather Station 2. While on station she was transferred to the Coast Guard. She departed Pearl Harbor on 20 June 1946 for San Francisco and on to Seattle for decommissioning on 12 August 1946. *Moberly* was struck from the Navy list on 23 April 1947 and sold for scrapping to Franklin

David Hendrickson

Shipwrecking Co. of Hillsdale, New Jersey, on 27 October 1947.

Upon conversion to weather ships at Boston in July 1945, *Key West* and *New Bedford* were destined to serve on station out of Guam in the far western Pacific. Both stopped briefly in Hawaii before proceeding west to Guam together, arriving in Apra Harbor on 10 September 1945. The assignment lasted until the end of February 1946, generally recognized as a time of grueling boredom, revealed by *Key West's* log: "Arrived Guam 10 Sept; sailed for station 14 Sept; returned to Guam 7 Oct; sailed for station 16 Oct; returned to Guam 1 Nov; sailed for station 8 Nov; returned to Guam 27 Nov; sailed for station 11 Dec; returned to Guam 31 Dec; sailed for last patrol 12 Jan; returned to Guam 9 Feb." *New Bedford* exchanged patrols with *Key West* until both departed for San Francisco via Pearl Harbor, arriving San Francisco in mid-March 1946. *New Bedford* proceeded to Seattle for decommissioning on 24 May 1946. *Key West* did a short spell of plane guard patrol on the California coast before sailing to Seattle and decommissioning on 14 June 1946. She was sold for scrap to Cascade Enterprises of Oakland, California, on 18 April 1947.

EJ Paso and *Racine* were bound for the Philippines for weather duty following conversion to weather ships in New York in July 1945. For *EJ Paso* it would be a return to unforgotten waters, for they arrived off Tacloban in Leyte Gulf on 23 September 1945, just short of one year since *EJ Paso* had seen her share of action in the invasion of Leyte beginning on 20 October 1944. On the 29th *Racine* proceeded to the island of Samar as her duty station. She worked from here until departing for Seattle on 14 April 1946 and decommissioning on 27 June. *Racine* was struck from the Navy list on 19 July 1946 and sold to Franklin Shipwrecking on 2 December 1947. The irony of *EJ Paso's* return to Leyte Gulf was that she had not suffered a scratch during action against the enemy but was close to being lost in a violent typhoon in November 1945. (See account to follow). With emergency repairs along the way at Subic Bay and Guam, she made it to Seattle for belated decommissioning on 18 July 1946 and finally to the breakers for scrapping on 14 October 1947.

It was left to *Corpus Christi* and *Hutchinson* as the last frigates to serve on active duty in the Pacific, and that service along the west coast of North America. Both had completed the long journey from western Australia to California in October 1945 for conversion to weather ships at Terminal Island. *Corpus Christi* was transferred to the Coast Guard and worked Weather Station "0" out of San Francisco until decommissioned on 2 August 1946. *Hutchinson* made for Seattle and two tours on Station Able, 6 February to 5 April 1946, then to San Francisco for two stints of plane guard duty until called for decommissioning on 23 September 1946. She went to Mexico in November 1947 and served the Mexican Navy as the *California*.

Report of events aboard USS EL PASO PF-41 during typhoon period 24-25 November 1945.

(a) Saturday, 24 November, 1945.

At 1200 this vessel on Weather Station "Sugar" was underway on a course of 26 degrees, speed six (6) knots, position by dead reckoning: Latitude 14° 38' N., Longitude 128° 38' E., with wind about two points on starboard bow, barometer reading 29.52. We were cruising in this direction in order to increase the distance from the reported path and center of the typhoon, travelling W.N.W. The sea was moderate, with winds of about twenty (20) knots. The wind continued to increase gradually and the ship's R.P.M.'s were also increased to maintain good steerageway. By 1430 the barometer had dropped to 29.18 and continuing to drop rapidly. The wind and sea from N.N.E. to N.E. was also increasing. By 1530 the wind and sea had increased to such an extent that it was impossible to keep the vessel's head up by any combination of engine speed and rudder. At 1600 the ship swung to port and despite all efforts, could not be brought back to course. The heading was about 315 degrees and the wind had increased to 60 to 70 knots from the N.E. All vents, hatches, ventilators on weather deck secured. At 1700 gave up the attempt to maneuver the vessel and as the course appeared to be carrying her in front of, or at least, parallel with the typhoon, the engines were stopped, with the expectation that the center of the typhoon would pass to the westward. Dispatch 240740 was sent advising as to situation. Except for the seas that swept the fantail the ship rode easily, with wind on the starboard quarter. The Loran had gone out of commission earlier in the day, and efforts to repair it failed. By 1800 the Radar was out due to water pouring through ventilators into the C.IC room. Practically all portholes, ventilators, bulkhead doors on the weather deck were leaking badly. Seas and winds continued to increase and the barometer to fall very rapidly. At 1915 running lights were secured due to short in panel board. Rolling and pitching increased as the ship neared the center of typhoon. Ship's furniture began tearing loose from bulkheads, water accumulated in the mess deck, officer's quarters, wardroom, sick bay, galley and radio room. At 2100 port generator burned out and all communication between bridge and engine room ceased except by messenger, which was extremely hazardous because of having to cross the weather deck in high winds and seas. Boiler fires went out about this time and attempts to re-light were unsuccessful, because of wind and water entering through the stack. An effort was made to send a message, but the transmitters were shorted out. TCY emergency lifeboat transmitter was put in operation, but of no practicable use, due to its short range. The vessel developed a 14 degree list to port. The average roll to port was about 40 to 50 degrees. Just prior to entering the eye of the storm, a roll of 62 degrees to port was noted. At about 2120 the ship entered the eye of the storm in the N.E. quadrant, barometer reading 26.90. The wind died rapidly, although seas were heavy. All hands turned to in clearing the vessel of a considerable amount of water, securing the mast that worked loose and otherwise trying to stop leaks in the weather decks. Two life rafts were swept away and several depth charges were lost overboard.

(b) Sunday, 25 November, 1945.

At about 0000 the ship again was caught in the wind, it is thought somewhere about the S.E. quadrant of the typhoon. Heavy winds and seas continued to about 0500, when it seemed as though the ship again entered the eye of the storm in the N.E. quadrant and leaving it at about 0630. The wind and seas were particularly violent to 0900, diminishing by about 1000 when we were apparently entering the eye of the storm. By 1100 the winds began to increase to gale force from the Northwest. The ship's head swung to about 170 degrees; the barometer, which had remained stationary at 26.90, started to rise rapidly and it reached 28.00 inches at 1300. All efforts were centered at this time on getting the vessel under power in an endeavor to maneuver it out of the storm area. However, due to the water down the stack, every attempt to light off the boiler failed. At 1500 wind shifted to westward and the ship's head fell off to about 140 degrees. Wind and seas continued at gale force and the barometer fell to 27.10. Instructions were issued to the engineer to use any available material on board to light off the boiler. Shoring timber,

48b

benches, books etc were used, and eventually the fires were touched off. At about 1945 the ship again entered a calm area. By 2140 a full head of steam was up and the ship was underway, set course 146 degrees by magnetic compass. Immediately after getting underway, encountered winds of gale force from the S.W., the barometer rising steadily.

(c) Monday, 26 November, 1845.

Continued on course 146 degrees until 0800, when course was changed to 180 degrees. At 1100 an unsatisfactory fix was obtained by observation of the sun. At noon, latitude sight was made, 14° 40' N. At 1345 fixed position at latitude 14° 27' N., longitude 128° 10' E. Changed course at 1645 for Suluan Light, P.I. Two radio receivers were working on the morning of the 26th, but no transmitters could be made operative. A sharp watch was kept for vessels that could relay a message. None were sighted except one so far away that it was impossible to signal her. At 1330 contact was made by voice circuit on 2716 K.C., and a report was made to CMOB, Samar. At 1630 stood into Guiuan Harbor and dropped anchor at 1705 off SRB, Manicani Island.

---

2.   The ship was battered and strained by the high winds and seas. Considerable damage was done to the hull, machinery, and ship's equipment. The ventilation system appears to be unsafe as some vents have no provision for closing. Water-tight doors, portholes, and ventilators could not be made water-tight and as a consequence the vessel shipped considerable amount of water through these openings, forcing the crew to labor with buckets in order to keep the vessel from becoming unstable. It is believed that it would have eventually contributed to the loss of the vessel should we have remained in the storm area.

3.   The anemometer carried away about 1730 on the 24th. The average wind velocity near center was believed to be 80 to 90 knots with gust up to 115 knots. An estimate of the drift of the vessel from time of loss of control to the time of getting underway was 210 miles, to the N.W. at an average of seven (7) knots. During the entire storm the wind and sea was always abaft the starboard beam, with the exception of the time in the eye of the storm, when the wind and sea, though heavy, was erratic.

4.   There were only minor injuries suffered by the personnel on board, one broken arm being the most serious. The crew were without cooked food for 48 hours. Their conduct at all times was exemplary, having worked without adequate food or sleep for long hours under most trying conditions.

Ed. note: In an exchange of letters in January 1970 between two retired officers, who were young men aboard El Paso during the storm, (Cmdr. Bryan Spencer and Cmdr. Alexander Cash), Spencer is pleased to share his tattered copy of the typhoon report with Cash. In his letter, Cash tells of the poor condition of PF-41 and the return to the States after Spencer left the ship. The ship had to be towed 300 miles to Guam after breaking down at sea after leaving Subic Bay. After repairs, on to Hawaii at 8 knots and on to Seattle for decommissioning. Anchored in Seattle, most of the crew and officers left, leaving Ensign Cash and a few enlisted men aboard. Apparently forgotten by the Navy in a removed anchorage, Cash finally took matters into hand, got up steam and docked PF-41 at Pier 88, and as Cash put it, ". . . much to the chagrin of the Navy there and I went to see the port Captain, who after several hours and with us holding up traffic got us a committment for decommissioning and a berth assignment at Bremerton Naval Shipyard. So I took the ship there without any problem and tied her up. We lay there more than three weeks before decommissioning orders arrived. . ." The battered wreck was decommissioned 18 July 1946.

Racine (PF-100) worked with *El Paso* on the Philippine weather and plane guard stations in late 1945 until mid-April 1946. George Bock, a plank owner aboard *Racine*, remembered the near loss of *El Paso* and the long tedious patrols out of Leyte and Samar. The following log records submitted by George follow *Racine's* Atlantic convoy duty to conversion as a weather ship and on to the Philippines and finally to Seattle for decommissioning:

6 July 1945 -- Moored starboard side to *Newport* (PF-27) at Navy docks, Tompkinsville, Staten Island, New York, for conversion to weather ship. After 3-inch gun and three 20mm guns removed and weather hanger installed.

7 August - 1655 --- underway enroute to Panama Canal in company with *El Paso* (PF-41).

13 August - 1346 --- anchored in Limon Bay, Canal Zone, in preparation for transit.

15 August - 0812 --- underway through locks with PF-41. 1740 moored to Pier 8, Balboa.

17 August - 1131 --- underway to Pearl Harbor in company with PF-41.

1 September - 1609 --- moored starboard side PF-41, US Naval anchorage, Pearl Harbor.

6 September - 1607 --- underway to Leyte, PI, in company with PF-41.

23 September - 1050 --- anchored in San Pedro Bay, Leyte, PI.

29 September - 1230 --- underway to Guiuan Bay, Samar, PI, for weather patrol and air sea rescue.

30 September to 29 November - - *Racine* exchanged seven patrols with PF-41 and PCE-844 on Station "Sugar" -- 14°N - 128° E. *Racine* rode out the typhoon of 24-26 November at anchor.

29 November - 1850 --- *El Paso* in battered condition moored to port side returning from Station "Sugar" and typhoon. Navy called off search for lost PF-41.

3 December to 21 December --- two patrols relieved by PCE 244 and DE-105. To Subic Bay for repairs 24 December.

8 January 1946 to 11 April--- *Racine* exchanged six patrols with PF-41, DE-764, PCE886

14 April - 1242 --- enroute to Pearl Harbor

18 April - 1123 --- arrive Apra Harbor, Guam. Received fuel from YO-186. 1458 depart for Hawaii.

30 April - 1330 --- moored in East Loch, Pearl Harbor.

3 May - 1308 --- underway for Seattle.

11 May - 1632 --- anchored in Elliott Bay, Seattle. *Orlando* (PF-99) moored to port.

11 May to 27 June 1946 --- at anchor at times moored to *Orlando, Gulfport, El Paso, Key West*. Decommissioned 27 June 1946. Of plank owners remaining aboard for decommissioning are the Captain, first lieutenant, two chief petty officers and five rated men.

486

Racine (PF-100) making for her last assignment -- weather duty in the Philippines

Entering Pearl Harbor, 1 September 1945

*Crew departing Racine.
Seattle, May 1946.*

Cooling off in the tropics

At the peak of wartime activity, twenty-two weather stations were patrolled in the Atlantic and twenty-four in the Pacific, all of which were the responsibility of the Navy except for nine Atlantic stations patrolled by the British and Brazilian Navies and one in the North Pacific patrolled by Canada. When the Navy announced in the spring of 1946 its intention of relinquishing responsibility for weather patrol in the Atlantic and eastern Pacific, the Coast Guard stepped in to work with the Weather Bureau, which believed strongly in the service and recommended the maintenance of twelve stations in the Atlantic and six between the Pacific Coast and the longitude of Hawaii. This was too ambitious a number for the Coast Guard to patrol with only nineteen frigates acquired from the Navy and limited available cutters at the same time that wartime personnel numbers were rapidly declining. The number of stations was reduced to a mere two in the Atlantic and three in the Pacific, and once the frigates were gone the Atlantic stations were assumed by the two Secretary-class cutters *Bibb* and *Spencer.* By the turn of the decade the station numbers had been settled at nine in the Atlantic and three in the Pacific. The Coast Guard maintained Bravo, Charlie, Delta and Echo in the western Atlantic, and European navies patrolled five stations from the Arctic south to a point west of the Bay of Biscay. In the Pacific, Canada patrolled the former Station Able in the Gulf Of Alaska and USCG cutters worked Stations November and Victor, located midway between San Francisco and Honolulu and midway between Honolulu and Tokyo, both on transoceanic air routes.

As quickly as the Navy decommissioned the Atlantic frigates, European nations geared up for acquiring needed weather patrol ships from the laid up list. *Sheboygan* went to Belgium in March 1947, *Abilene* and *Forsyth* to The Netherlands in May and July 1947. When France agreed to maintain two of the eastern Atlantic stations, four frigates were purchased in March 1947 and reconditioned in New Orleans before making for Brest and final preparation as meteorological vessels. The four new weather frigates were *Laplace (ex-Lorain), Mermoz* (ex *Muskegon), Brix (ex-Manitowoc)* and *Verrier (ex-Emporia).* All four were home ported at Brest and served alternately on Point "L" west of Ireland and Point "K" west of the Bay of Biscay at 45°N -16° W. The four newly acquired weather ships served the French Navy until 1952, all but *Laplace,* which was lost in 1950. Gerry Harris of *Lorain* pursued the story of the loss of his former ship after reading in U.S. Warships of World War II of the *Lorain* being sold to France in 1947 and lost 16 September 1950. In a letter to Patrol Frigate Reunion Association (PFRA), July 1997, Gerry wrote:

> ... For a long time, I pondered the meaning of the word "lost." Did it mean the ship was sunk in battle, or perhaps in a storm? Eventually, curiosity got the better of me, and I wrote a letter to the French Embassy in Washington in 1990. The Embassy forwarded the inquiry to the French Naval Ministry, and the needed information was sent to me December 27, 1990, by Pierre Waksman, Chief of Naval Historical Service...

The loss of *Laplace* occurred on the night of 15-16 September 1950 while lying at anchor off St. Malo, France. En route to her home port, Brest, from a twenty-one day tour at Point K, *Laplace* proceeded to St. Malo to participate in the inauguration ceremonies of the Great Lock scheduled for Saturday, 16 September. She anchored 900 meters offshore in fifteen meters of water. Shortly after midnight a violent explosion shook the vessel. The ship was plunged into darkness and in an estimated eight to eleven minutes capsized and sank. Of the ninety-two men on board, fifty-two were lost. The Navy established a commission of enquiry. Divers examined the broken hull and concluded that the sinking was caused by a German mine, long embedded in the mud and no doubt detonated by the anchor chain as the ship swung with the tide.

Weather frigate *Brix* was withdrawn from service on 10 July 1952. In five years of duty she counted twenty-two patrols of one month each at Points "L" and "K," several good will missions to French coastal towns as a representative of the Navy, 630 days at sea, 57,600 miles of travel and one long period in dry-dock in the port of La Pallice from January to March 1952. She was returned to the Minister of Public Works and broken up at Brest in 1956 after years of being laid up and cannibalized for parts. Apparently, the *ex-Muskegon* and *ex-Emporia* ended up on the scrap heap in the mid-1950s.

Colombia acquired three frigates, *Groton* bought at disposal by the State Department at New Orleans, 26 March 1947, and *Bisbee* and *Burlington* acquired at Yokosuka, Japan, following US Navy service in the Korean War. All three served in the Korean conflict flying Colombian colors but under orders of the United States Navy. *Almirante Padilla (ex-Groton)* was scrapped in 1965. *Capitan Tono (ex-Bisbee)* and *Almirante Biron (ex-Burlington)* went to the breakers in 1962.

Almirante Padilla left Colombia for San Diego and major repairs before steaming on to Yokosuka, arriving 30 April 1951, to be placed under the operational control of the Commander of Force Unit 5, her record and those of her sisters accounted for in a Colombian naval article "La Guerra de Corea" (The Korean War):

> ... During its stay in the Far East, the frigate *Almirante Padilla* brilliantly carried out all of its assigned combat missions under the unified command of the U.N. as, for example, to escort supply shipments, to bombard coasts and to destroy enemy supply lines, and to blockade the port of Wonsan and the enemy coast until it officially ended participation in the conflict on January 19, 1952 and received orders to return to Colombia...

Bisbee went to Colombia on 12 February 1952. As the newly christened *Capitan Tono* she underwent intensive training and trials until put under operational command in Sasebo. On 1 May 1952 she carried out her first war assignment as escort of supply ships to the east coast of Korea and remained on station to participate in coastal bombardment. On 5 November she moored in Pusan for a visit to the U.N. cemetery to render homage to the

Colombians who fell in war action. Her war mission completed on 27 January 1953, *Capitan Tono* returned to Colombia.

50a

Capitán de Corbeta
Julio César Reyes Canal,
Comandante del ARC
"Almirante Padilla".

El ARC "Almirante Padilla" navegando con rumbo al Lejano Oriente.

ex-*Groton* (PF-29)

The ARC "Admiral Padilla" sailing toward the Far East.

La tripulación del ARC "Almirante Padilla" en vísperas de su zarpe de San Diego hacia mares del Lejano Oriente.

The crew of the ARC "Admiral Padillo" on the eve of sailing from San Diego to the Far East

50b

ARC "Capitán Tono".

ex-Bisbee (PF-46)

ARC "Almirante Brion".

ex-Burlington (PF-51)

50c

Frigate captains of the Colombian Navy

Capitán de Corbeta Carlos Prieto Silva, Comandante ARC "Almirante Brion".

Capitán de Corbeta Hernando Berón Victoria, Comandante ARC "Capitán Tono".

Regresa victoriosa la Fragata ARC "Capitán Tono".

The frigate ARC "Capitan Tono" victoriously returns

A number of Tacoma-class ships served extended careers abroad. Here Eugene is seen in 1955 as the Cuban Jose Marti. Official USN Photograph. The ship was transferred to Cuba on 16 June 1947.

50e

USS *Bisbee* (PF-46)

U.S.S. NEWPORT

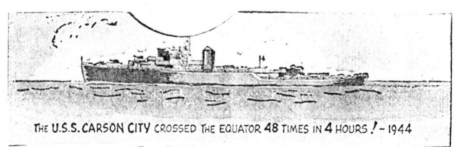

THE U.S.S. CARSON CITY CROSSED THE EQUATOR 48 TIMES IN 4 HOURS ! – 1944

From Bob Ripley's *Believe It Or Not*

Almirante Biron was officially transferred to Colombia on 26 June 1953 at Yokosuka, and following intensive training, set sail for Sasebo on 18 July. On 29 July she received her first order as an escort for supplies to a point near Wonsan. On 11 September she lowered her motor whaleboat for the successful rescue of a Korean sailor overboard from the frigate *Duman (ex-Muskogee)*. While raising the boat, an accident claimed the life of machinist Hector Perea Vallojes. On 22 April 1954, upon being relieved by the return of *Capitan Tono*, *Almirante Biron* set sail from Yokosuka for Colombia.

The return of vessels loaned to the Soviet Union at Cold Bay under Project Hula in summer 1945 became a sticky issue resulting from strained relations between the two countries in post-war years. And as conditions developed it is not puzzling that the final agreement "Settlement of Lend Lease, Reciprocal Aid and Claims" was not reached until 18 October 1972. The United States first raised the issue of settling obligations in February 1946, pointing to Article V of the Master Lend-Lease Agreement of 11 June 1942:

> The Government of the Union of Soviet Socialist Republics will return to the United States of America at the end of the present emergency, as determined by the President of the United States of America, such defense articles transferred under this agreement as shall not have been destroyed, lost or consumed and shall be determined by the President to be useful in the defense of the United States of America or of the Western Hemisphere or to be otherwise of use to the United States of America.

With the agreement in mind, Secretary of the Navy James V. Forrestal on 8 May 1947 informed the State Department that the Navy wanted 480 of the 585 combatants in Soviet hands returned. On 4 June 1947, Secretary of State George C. Marshall replied that the Navy's demand would create more trouble than it was worth. While the Navy never abandoned its efforts to obtain a settlement for all vessels, Forrestal did agree to a curtailed list focused on three Wind-class icebreakers (not Hula Project vessels) and the twenty-eight *Tacoma*-class frigates. An agreement was not reached until 1948, when the Soviets announced approximate dates for return of the frigates and the icebreakers. In October and November 1949, twenty-seven frigates, less ex-*Belfast* reported a total loss from storm damage, discarded their EK numbers and were returned to the US Navy at Yokosuka, Japan. Most experienced Navy hands who viewed the decrepit and rusted assembly bobbing side by side at distant mooring buoys, wished they would go away, disappear and go to sea and sink. Little thought was given to their recommissioning. The Korean War was seven months away.

North Korean troops poured across the 38th Parallel on 25 June 1950. The war was on, and in the face of a badly depleted fleet, the frigates moored close to the scene of war became immediate candidates for reactivation. Fifteen were chosen: five Kaiser products: *Tacoma, Sausalito, Albuquerque, Everett, Hoquiam;* six Consolidated Steel ships, *Glendale,*

Gallup, Bisbee, Burlington, Muskogee, Rockford; four Great Lakes ships, *Newport, Bayonne, Evansville, Gloucester.*

51a

David Hendrickson

51b

PATROL FRIGATES OF THE KOREAN WAR

RECOMMISSIONING SCHEDULE

25 JUN 1950 --- North Korean forces cross the 38th parallel. Hostilities begin at 4:00 a.m.

Fifteen *Tacoma*-class patrol frigates moored in red lead row at U.S. Navy Fleet Activities, Yokosuka, Japan, chosen for reactivation for blockade and escort service with Task Force 95 and Task Force 77 and commissioned as follows:

26 JUL 1950 --- USS EVERETT (PF-8)
27 JUL 1950 --- USS NEWPORT (PF-27)
28 JUL 1950 --- USS BAYONNE (PF-21)
29 JUL 1950 --- USS EVANSVILLE (PF-70)
15 SEP 1950 --- USS SAUSALITO (PF-4)

> United Nations forces landed at INCHON, 15 SEP 1950. NEWPORT, BAYONNE and EVANSVILLE participated in escort and gunfire support of the assault force.

27 SEP 1950 --- USS HOQUIAM (PF-5)
 3 OCT 1950 --- USS ALBUQUERQUE (PF-7)
11 OCT 1950 --- USS GLENDALE (PF-36)
11 OCT 1950 --- USS GLOUCESTER (PF-22)
18 OCT 1950 --- USS GALLUP (PF-47)
18 OCT 1950 --- USS BISBEE (PF-46)

23 OCT 1950 --- USS MUSKOGEE (PF-49)   Loaned to ROK Navy
23 OCT 1950 --- USS ROCKFORD (PF-48)   Loaned to ROK Navy

1 DEC 1950   --- USS TACOMA (PF-3)
5 JAN 1951 --- USS BURLINGTON (PF-51)

Twelve frigates remained in inactive service at Yokosuka and were later transferred to Japan for service in the Japanese Maritime Safety Administration.

USS PASCO (PF-6)
USS CHARLOTTESVILLE (PF-25)
USS POUGHKEEPSIE (PF-26)
USS LONG BEACH (PF-34)
USS SAN PEDRO (PF-37)
USS CORONADO (PF-38)
USS OGDEN (PF-39)
USS CARSON CITY (PF-50)
USS ALLENTOWN (PF-52)
USS MACHIAS (PF-53)
USS SANDUSKY (PF-54)
USS BATH (PF-55)

USS Tacoma (PF-3) freshly reactivated for the Korean War, Yokosuka, Japan, Spring 1951.

51d

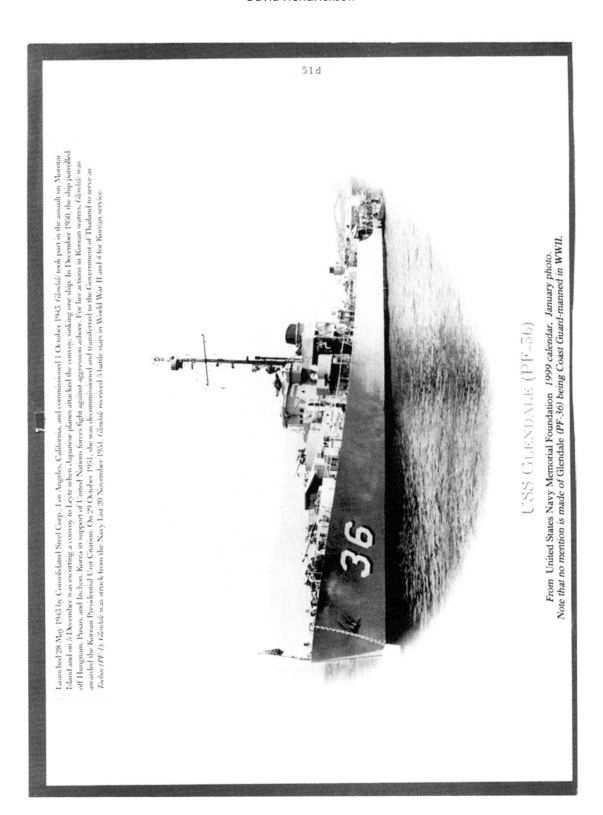

Launched 28 May 1943 by Consolidated Steel Corp., Los Angeles, California, and commissioned 1 October 1943. *Glendale* took part in the assault on Morotai Island and on 5 December was escorting a convoy to Leyte when Japanese planes attacked the convoy, sinking one ship. In December 1950, the ship patrolled off Hungnam, Pusan, and Inchon, Korea in support of United Nations forces fight against aggression ashore. For her actions in Korean waters, *Glendale* was awarded the Korean Presidential Unit Citation. On 29 October 1951, she was decommissioned and transferred to the Government of Thailand to serve as *Tahin (PF-1)*. *Glendale* was struck from the Navy List 20 November 1951. *Glendale* received 5 battle stars in World War II and 4 for Korean service.

USS GLENDALE (PF-36)

From United States Navy Memorial Foundation 1999 calendar, January photo.
Note that no mention is made of Glendale (PF-36) being Coast Guard-manned in WWII.

51e

USS *Albuquerque* (PF-7) -- drawing by Korean War crewman

51f

COMMANDER
UNITED NATIONS BLOCKADING AND ESCORT FORCE
PUBLIC INFORMATION OFFICE

PRESS RELEASE

FOR IMMEDIATE RELEASE __X__   HOLD FOR RELEASE UNTIL _____
SUBMITTED: __23 June 1952__   SOURCE: __INTERVIEW__
APPROVED: ____X____   WRITTEN BY: __D. S. MANNISON, JO3__
FORWARDED: _____   CHECKED BY: __LT. J.C. SWEENEY__

FIGHTING DIPLOMATS
OF USS ALBUQUERQUE

"Diplomats who fight" is the motto of the small patrol frigate
USS ALBUQUERQUE.

The Navy ship, named for the city of Albuquerque, New Mexico,
recently completed a five month tour of duty at Hong Kong, where
it worked in close liaison with the American Naval Attache in
the British Crown Colony.

The trim fighting frigate Albuquerque, and the 189 officers
and men comprising her crew soon proved in the Korean combat
area that their fighting powers was not an empty boast.

During her first action in waters off the Communist-held
Korea last month, the frigate ranged the North Korean east coast,
from Hungnam to Songjin, firing almost continuously for nine
days on enemy military installations and positions.

At Wonsan, where United Nations naval forces have maintained
a continuous blockade for more than a year, the Albuquerque's three-
inch rifles blasted at supply centers, ammunition dumps and troop
concentrations.

Closing the range between her guns and the enemy targets, she
ventured deep into Wonsan harbor. Concealed Communist shore batteries began blasting away at the Albuquerque, and during the en-
suing gun duel, six enemy shells landed close to the ship.

Although the Albuquerque suffered no direct hits, shrapnel
from a projectile exploding twenty yards from the ship injured
one man. While manning a forty-millimeter gun mount and blasting at nearby enemy sampans, Commissaryman First Class Harold J.
Graff, USN, of Marshall, Texas received shrapnel wounds in the
shoulder.

A few days later, the Albuquerque was firing on supply dumps
and railway bridges at Hungnam, and also supplying fire support
coverage while tiny minesweepers patrolled the harbor. At Hungnam, the ship was once again bracketed by Communist shore batt-
teries. When the Albuquerque steamed out of the Hungnam area, it
left a railway marshalling yard in flames as a fiery reminder of
her presence.

During the Albuquerque's first nine days of combat, her three
3-inch guns barked often, and the enemy felt the not-so-diplomatic
sting of over 2,500 rounds of high explosive projectiles.

Burlington *preparing to pass wounded North Korean prisoner by stretcher and highline to cruiser St. Paul, Sea of Japan, winter 1951.*

Heavy weather damage to forward 3-inch gun tub, Korean War, winter 1951

Hedgehog and depth charges

David Hendrickson

51h

HEADQUARTERS
COMMANDER NAVAL FORCES FAR EAST
PUBLIC INFORMATION OFFICE

FOR IMMEDIATE RELEASE   May 17, 1951

A group of frigates, returned to the United States by Russia
following World War II in a condition far below standards usually
exacted by the U.S. Navy, have been daily doing an emergency job
for the United Nations in Korean waters deserving of praise for the
ships and their crews.

The small escort bombardment ships have been an increasingly
vital factor in maintenance of the 10-month naval blockade of the
enemy's east and west coast. Their three inch batteries have joined
those of the mighty USS MISSOURI, the cruiser MANCHESTER, ST. PAUL
and HELENA in the harbors of Wonsan and Songjin. Both of these key
rail and highway centers on Korea's northeast coast land supply route
to the central front have been under continuous navy siege for over
two months - exceeding the historic siege of Vicksburg in 1863 by
many weeks.

The blockade effort along the enemy's east and west coast has
been almost 100% effective since it went into effect by Presidential
proclamation July 4, 1950, a few days after tank-tipped North Korean
Communist armies smashed across the 38th parallel to invade the
Republic of Korea.

Immediately the naval blockade knocked out three of the enemy's
five main supply routes. The first was the junk and steamer routes
from the Siberian border southward to the front-lines. The second
was the coastal junk and shallow water route down the Yellow Sea from
the Yalu river to the battle line. The third was the route across
the Yellow Sea from Asiatic ports to Chinnampo, Haeju, Sinanju and
other Korean ports on the west coast of the peninsula. The shallow
draft frigates have assisted greatly in keeping these sea-lanes cut,
and at the same time they have darted in to strike at a fourth communist main supply route - the northeast rail and highway network
along the east coast. A fifth main supply route, that from Antung in
Communist China leading down to Pyongyang and southward to the Seoul
area is out of ships' gun range and is being hammered day and night
by Air Force and Navy planes.

Not only have the frigates done their work in the offensive
operations of the naval war, but several participated in the massive
seaborne redeployment of the United Nations forces last December and
January when our armies recoiled from the onslaught of hundreds of
thousands of newly committed and fresh Chinese Communist troops.

One of the Task Force 95 frigates, the USS GLOUCESTER assisted
in both the withdrawal from Wonsan and Hungnam on the east coast in
December, and later at Inchon on the other side of the peninsula in
early January. Commanded by Lieut. Comdr. Thomas C. Clay, USN, of
622 Drayton St., Savannah, Ga., the GLOUCESTER dropped its anchor in
Wonsan harbor and served as a harbor entrance control vessel to
guide newly arrived landing craft and transports to their proper
loading berths during withdrawal operation at that port. Later,
the frigate moved north to Hungnam where it assisted in the stupen-
dous task of redeploying an entire army and all its equipment by sea.
During that dramatic operation when the nation held its breath ex-
pecting a bloody "Dunkirk" of unmatched proportions 5,000 miles from
its home shores. Naval forces extricated 105,000 soldiers and

marines, 91,000 liberty loving Koreans and their scant belongings, and over 350,000 tons of vitally needed military equipment and supplies, plus 17,500 vehicles. Nothing was left for the Red hordes. The GLOUCESTER and other frigates assisted in that great operation.

The GLOUCESTER later moved to the west coast of Korea where her shallow draft (about twelve feet) made it an excellent vessel for anti-junk and blockade patrols along the enemy's muddy and treacherous west coast. It was there during the U.N. withdrawal from Inchon in January that the GLOUCESTER picked up 30 North Korean refugees - men, women and children that had made their bid for freedom on the open seas and had won - thanks to the U.S. frigate and her crew. Adrift in their dilapidated junk the Koreans were taken aboard the GLOUCESTER, given baths, hot meals, and the warmth of human kindness inherent in all good sailors. The youngest of the tragic lot was an infant - age 1 month. The refugees, with their junk in tow, were taken to Kunsan in South Korea by the American frigate.

After its first patrol the GLOUCESTER put into port at the big U.S. Naval Base at Yokosuka, Japan. As its recently recalled executive officer, Lieut. John H. Mulski, USNR, explained, "We all needed rest and got it at Yokosuka where the whole crew was able to spend a few days at one of the Armed Forces rest hotels." Lt. Mulski returned to duty in September, 1950, from New York City where he was a member of Naval Reserve Organized Surface Division 3-51. His home is 14 Stuyvesant Oval, N.Y.C.

Another frigate that's been around a lot is the USS BURLINGTON. The 300 foot man-o-war recently completed its first combat patrol in Korean waters along the enemy's east coast where it carried out numerous blockade patrols, and also participated in the siege bombardments of Wonsan and Songjin.

Commanded by Lieut. Comdr. James F. Moore, USNR, of Bunker Hill, Ind., who is also a former radio newscaster of station KRIC in Beaumont, Tex., the BURLINGTON is manned by an all-Reserve officer complement and a 95% Reserve enlisted crew.

During its first blockade patrol the BURLINGTON steamed over 5,000 miles carrying out its ceaseless missions, and fired hundreds of rounds of three-inch high explosive shells into enemy defenses, transportation targets, rolling stock, and military installations at Wonsan, Chaho, Songjin, and Chongjin, only 50 miles from the Siberian boarder.

March 24, 1951, at Songjin the BURLINGTON fired some 100 rounds into enemy supply dumps, a railroad trestle, and boxcars. A number of boxcars were destroyed by the frigates' accurate gunfire. Earlier, down the coast at Wonsan, Lt. Comdr. Moore and his Naval Reserve crew took part in a surprise shelling of enemy troop concentrations that is reported to have caused 8,000 casualties in eight minutes of concentrated gunfire.

Recently commended by Rear Admiral Allan E. Smith, USN, commander of the United Nations Blockading and Escort Force (Task Force 95), for its excellent performance during six weeks at sea, "Skipper" Moore explained that his formula for keeping the BURLINGTON ready for action was to insist on complete lubrication of all working machinery, making the ship's engines a living concern of his engineering crew, and careful observation of maintenance work by yard overhaul crews. While the temporary flagship of Admiral Smith enroute from Wonsan, Korea to a Japanese port, the little frigate maintained a cruising speed of 15½ knots for 22 hours which attested to the success of Moore's formula.

Other frigates are beginning to make themselves known as fighting ships to be reckoned with by the enemy. The USS HOQUIAM has added her punch to that of other siege ships at Songjin, and has often raided in the Chongjin area of far North Korea. The ship has been on the prowl in Korean waters since April 2nd.

Returned by the Russians after World War II and anchored at Yokosuka harbor awaiting further disposition by the U.S. Navy, the frigates were placed in service a few months after the U.N. action in Korea commenced. The U.S. Navy needed more ships in both the Pacific and the Mediteranean to cope with Communist designs for aggression. The frigates were on the scene in the Far East, and being seaworth, were drafted into service. The naval action in Korean waters involved only a short day or two of cruising from Japanese ports. Much of the action and blockade effort was on the west coast where the water is shallow, and the need for light draft patrol vessels is great. The frigates filled the bill.

Life on the 1430-ton ships is not comfortable by civilian standards, but the frigates are roomy. All the crews enjoy nightly movies at sea, the usual shipboard reading facilities, and other limited personal comforts. Moving about the ship is not as difficult as aboard a destroyer, nor as dangerous as aboard a minesweeper. The ships get into port more often than do cruisers, carriers, and destroyers; thus, affording more opportunities for rest and recreation ashore. Gradually the kinks in the equipment caused by the Russian lack of proper maintenance are being ironed out or replaced entirely.

The main thing is that the frigates are doing an important job. Their crews are getting their sealegs back after years of civilian life as inactive reservists. The fact the ships are coming into their own is a credit to the many civilian sailors, who took what was available in an emergency and are making fighting ships out of neglected but basically good vessels.

-30-

The Patrol Frigate Story

51k

Mail Call

USS EVERETT PF-8 on station in Hong Kong, 1953

The Last Command To Serve The USS EVERETT PF-8

Dear Ed:

In reference to your PF (Patrol Frigate) article. In the Fall of 1950, Yokosuka, Japan, we, the USS McKEAN DD-784 and three other destroyers came to port for a little R & R & repairs. Upon arrival we observed 40 rusty-green, stinking, floating, pile of crud anchored in the harbor. We were advised they were American Frigates that were returned by the Russians.

I remembered making this statement, "I sure feel sorry for anyone getting assigned to those ships." As you may have guessed, in the summer of 1952 I was assigned to the USS EVERETT PF-8, which was on station with Task Force 77 on the Yellow Sea, shielding the carriers just as the destroyers were doing.

They went on plane guard, received fire from shore batteries and if you have never stood the mid-watch in the forward gun tub during a driving rainstorm, you've never sailed.

I was on two destroyers (McKEAN-CHEVALIER) and the EVERETT and I assure you the PFs were every bit a Tin Can as a Tin Can **can** be.

I was very glad when we went back to our assigned station which was in Hong Kong as a Station Ship with the U.S. Embassy.

In 1953 we returned to Yokosuka and turned the ship over to the South Korean Navy and I was assigned to the CHEVALIER DDR-805. In the year I served aboard the EVERETT I only saw one other PF and it was the number 7 and I can't remember her name but we relieved her in Hong Kong.

There is one stat you left out, but I believe the Frigates could carry 202 thousand gallons of fuel, a hell of a lot more than a destroyer.

The EVERETT not only was named for a city, it was actually built there, (Everett, Washington.)

For the good of the American Navy, I sure hope no other navy has to go aboard a ship returned by the Russian Navy.

Fraternally,
Verner L. Newman III
1708 Ohio,
Lawrence, KS. 66044

158

Refurbished throughout and dressed up in new paint, a tilted cap affixed atop her stack affording a rakish look and finished off with a large white number 8 on her bow, *Everett* was first to be commissioned, 26 July 1950. *Burlington* treated in like fashion was the last of the fifteen commissioned, 5 January 1951.

Bayonne got underway from Kobe on 11 September 1950 to participate in the Inchon landings, followed quickly by her sister *Newport* on 15 September. A principal assignment for many of the frigates was escort, patrol and at times bombardment in the Wonsan area of the east coast of North Korea. *Gloucester* and *Everett* suffered casualties from shore fire while bombarding on the north coast and *Hoquiam* had to retire to Yokosuka for repairs earned in an exchange with an enemy shore battery. On occasion chosen ships steamed far afield to Subic Bay, Hong Kong, and places like Saigon, Bangkok and Singapore on goodwill tours. The old Bering Sea veterans, *Albuquerque* and *Everett,* relieved each other on long stays as station ship for the US consulate in Hong Kong. An excess of forty battle stars were earned by the fifteen frigates by the time *Everett,* the last to leave the fleet, was decommissioned on 10 March 1953.

All twenty-seven of the former Lend Lease vessels, except for *Bisbee* and *Burlington* that went to Colombia, were transferred to Asian allies: eighteen to Japan, five to the Republic of Korea and two to Thailand. At long last the Navy could breathe a sigh of relief, a gang of ships never quite accepted by Navy brass, parceled off to the Coast Guard during WWII and now the last of them in other hands scattered around Asia. Not quite as unseaworthy as some thought, the likes of former trouble-plagued *Tacoma* served the ROK Navy as *Taedong* (PF-63) until 28 February 1973. Her name was struck from the Navy list on 2 April 1973, and she was then donated to the ROK Navy as a museum and training ship.

Art Wells of the *Belfast* wartime crew in the Southwest Pacific and Cold Bay transfer to the USSR pursued the story of the loss of the the ship by the Russians. In an exchange of letters with Richard Russell, author of the Naval Historical Center publication Project Hula, Russell described meeting with Russian naval historian Sergei S. Berezhnoi. He passed on to Art his translation of Berezhnoi's account of the *Belfast* that appeared in the historian's book on Lend Lease ships:

> ... on 12 July 1945 accepted by a Soviet crew from the allies in accordance with lend lease, departing Cold Bay on 15 July 1945 and arriving on 23 July 1945 at Petropavlovsk Kamchatskii for inclusion with the Soviet Pacific Ocean Fleet. .. Participated in the Great Patriotic War: landings at Seishin (Chongchin) and Genzan (Wonsan) on 15 August and 21 August 1945, defense of communications and bases, and convoy service. From 16 November 1945 included in the Sakhalin Military Flotilla and from 17 January 1947 until 23 April 1953 in the Soviet 7th Fleet. On 18 December 1948, while operating in the Korsakov area off Sakhalin Island, damaged in a

storm and run aground. Through the efforts of fire and damage control, returned to port to repair hole in the hull. From 31 December 1952 excluded from order of battle, disarmed and converted into a floating base and on 27 December 1956 a floating barracks, but on 29 April 1960 excluded from the Navy's official list of ships in connection with transfer to the section of excess property for scrapping and, from 18 June 1960, dismantled.

52a

The Evansville (PF-70) in later years as the Japanese Keyaki. *Official USN Photograph, taken on or shortly before 9 Aug. 1962. The ship was transferred to Japan on 31 Oct. 1953.*

Eighteen Tacoma-class frigates, renamed for Japanese trees, served the Japanese Coastal Security Force as Tree-class frigates until replaced by larger ex-American warships in the 1960s.

KASHI (ex-USS PASCO (PF-6)
KAYA (ex-USS SAN PEDRO (PF-37)
KUSU (ex-USS OGDEN (PF-39)
MAKI (ex-USS CHARLOTTESVILLE (PF-25)
MOMI (ex-USS POUGHKEEPSIE (PF-26)
NARA (ex-USS MACHIAS (PF-53)
NIRE (ex-USS SANDUSKY (PF-54)
SUGI (ex-USS CORONADO (PF-38)
UMI (ex-USS ALLENTOWN (PF-52)
   (ex-USS ALBUQUERQUE (PF-7) *TOCHI*
   (ex-USS BAYONNE (PF-21) *BUNA*
   (ex-USS BATH (PF-55) *MATSU*
   (ex-USS NEWPORT (PF-27) *KAEDE*
   (ex-USS CARSON CITY (PF-50) *SAKURA*
   (ex-USS EVANSVILLE (PF-70) *KEYAKI*
   (ex-USS EVERETT (PF-8) *KIRI*
   (ex-USS GLOUCESTER (PF-22) *TSUGE*
   (ex-USS LONG BEACH (PF-34) *SHII*

Displacement: 1430 tons (2100 tons full load)
Dimensions: 304 (o.a.) x 37-1/2 x 37-1/2 x 13-1/2 (max.)
   feet
Guns: Three 3-inch, .50-Cal. d.p., ten 40mm and 20mm AA
Machinery: Triple expansion. 2 shafts. IHP: 5500 = 20 kts.
Complement: 180

PF「かや」ありし日の姿

PF KAYA IN HER LAST DAYS

写真提供：市栄 正樹／佐藤 兵衛／海上自衛隊／編集部

52b

Former USS San Pedro (PF-37)

Photo taken on March 17, 1970 as the *Kaya* was leaving Kobe Harbor. Ship was leased to the MSDF on March 30, 1953 under the US-Japan Agreement for Lease of Ships. On August 28, 1962 *Kaya* was turned over to the Japanese Maritime Self Defense Force and designated a support ship for the antisubmarine operations on December 10, 1963, assigned to the First Submarine Group, the predecessor of the First Antisubmarine Flotilla. From March 31,1972 until struck from the registry on April 1, 1979, she was an anchored training ship at the Sasebo Training Unit. *Kaya* became the target ship for the ASM-1, developed by the Japanese Defense Agency and sunk on June 13, 1979.

52 c

USS Albuquerque PF-7   Note from duty during Korean War 1951-53

Each night, the Albuquerque patrolled an assigned section of the enemy-held coast, ever watchful for signs of troop activity or supply movement.

Being close to Communist areas of activity was not a new thing for the crew of the Albuquerque. While at Hong Kong they were constantly within twelve miles of Red territory.

"At Hong Kong the ship was fully dressed every day-flags and all," remarked the Albuquerque's skipper, LtDlg. Walter L. Rhinehart USNR, of Washington, D. C., "But in Korea we were also fully dressed--dressed for battle and ready for action."

LCDR, Rhinehart is not a stranger to the intracacies of international protocol. Before being recalled to active duty he was Deputy Director of Personnel for the Mutual Security Agency in Washington.

During the Albuquerque's first nine days of combat, her three 3-inch guns barked often, and the enemy felt the not-so-diplomatic sting of over 2,500 rounds of high explosive projectiles.

As the post-World War II and Korean War years rolled on, the chance opportunity of a former frigate sailor ever again seeing one of the *Tacoma*-class ships was slim to nil. Few frigates ventured far from the ports of new owners, be it Cuba, Mexico or Thailand, and by the end of the 1950s most of those owned by Latin American countries were laid up or headed for scrapping. The twenty-seven frigates flying the flags of Japan, Korea and Thailand sailed respective coastal waters well into the 1960s and beyond. By the mid-60s Japan had retired ten as permanently moored training vessels, several were chosen for sinking as target ships and others decommissioned or returned to the United States in 1970. Of the five frigates under ROK colors, *Apnok (ex-Rockford),* severely damaged in a collision was returned to the U.S. Navy, 3 September 1952, then swung at anchor in a rusting condition until towed to sea and sunk as a torpedo target, 30 September 1953. *Sausalito* as *Imchin* along with *ex-Muskogee, ex-Hoquiam* and ex-*Tacoma* flew the ROK flag into the 1970s.

The surprise opportunity to climb aboard for a brief visit to their old wartime frigates fell to active USCG officers, Thomas Sargent and Kenneth Wilson in 1955 and 1956 respectively. Presently V. Adm. (Ret), then Cmdr. Sargent has recalled, "In 1955, while I was in Yokosuka Naval Base, Japan, *as* CO of the *Winnebago* (W-40), I noticed a few frigates tied up. By asking operations, I found the *Sandusky* and went aboard. The Japanese OD was at first reluctant but relented. I went to the bridge and just thought and reminisced about the great ship, the outstanding crew and what a joy it had been to have Command," In 1956, Lt. Cmdr. Wilson, Captain of the Port, Honolulu, and former gunnery officer on the *San Pedro*, watched two ships bearing Japanese flags enter the Port of Honolulu. "It was a strange feeling," Wilson recalled, "no one could miss the vertical mast and stack of the patrol frigates. It was even stranger when I made my official call aboard the flagship, the *Kaya*, and the commanding officer told me it was the former American ship USS *San Pedro.*" They're all gone now, save for the *ex-Glendale* and *ex-Gallup,* as noted earlier, as far as is known still flying the colors of the Royal Thai Navy in the late 1990s. We leave it to the aging American former Coast Guard and Navy crewmen of these gallant vessels to investigate and report back to the old sailors of the not quite "Forgotten Fleet."

END

Bibliography

HISTORY OF THE UNITED STATES NAVAL OPERATIONS IN WORLD WAR II, 15 Vol., 1947-1962, Samuel Eliot Morison.

    Vol. 7 Aleutians, Gilberts and Marshalls, June 1942 -April 1944

    Vol. 8 New Guinea and the Marianas, March 1944 -August 1944

    Vol. 12 Leyte, June 1944 -January 1945

    Vol. 13 The Liberation of the Philippines -Luzon, Mindanao, The Visayas, 1944 -1945

GUARDIANS OF THE SEA -A History of the U.S. Coast Guard 1915 to the Present, Robert Erwin Johnson, Naval Institute Press, 1987, .

THE U.S. COAST GUARD IN WORLD WAR II, Malcolm F. Willoughby, Naval Institute Press, 1957.

PROJECT HULA -Secret Soviet-American Cooperation in the War Against Japan, Richard A. Russell, No.4 The U.S. Navy in the Modem World Series, Naval Historical Center, Department of the Navy, Washington, 1997.

Dictionary of AMERICAN NAVAL FIGHTING SHIPS, 9 Vol.

WAR DIARIES --Patrol Frigates of World War II.

ALLIED ESCORT VESSELS OF WORLD WAR II -Royal Navy

"*Patrol Frigates*," Conways --All the World's Fighting Ships 1922-1946.

"*The Tacoma-class Frigates of World War II*," Robert Erwin Johnson, Warship International No.2, 1992.

"*Six Months with the Seventh Fleet*," Robert Erwin Johnson, The American Neptune -Maritime History and Arts, Vol. 57, No.3, Summer 1997.

"*Coast Guard-Manned Naval Vessels in World War II*," Robert Erwin Johnson, Commandant's Bulletin, February 1993.

Lightning Source UK Ltd.
Milton Keynes UK
UKHW030637070223
416609UK00013B/3092

9 780984 637102